The Velocity Advantage

Jack Bergstrand

Second Edition

Brand Velocity Inc.

© 2017 Jack Bergstrand

ISBN-10: 0692753869

ISBN-13: 978-0692753866

Library of Congress Control Number: 2016917922
LCCN Imprint Name: Brand Velocity Inc., Atlanta, Georgia

Brand Velocity, Strategic Profiling, and Consequent are
registered trademarks of Brand Velocity Inc.

*When the increase in velocity is great enough,
the very nature of business changes.*

**—Bill Gates,
Business @ the Speed of Thought**

Table of Contents

Why Read The Velocity Advantage?

SENIOR EXECUTIVES

- **Better and faster outcomes:** Make velocity a sustainable competitive advantage for your organization.
- **Higher employee engagement:** Help people to be their best to make a meaningful and lasting difference.
- **Leadership development:** Help employees reach their potential by adopting a shared language and approach.

MANAGERS

- **Practical insights:** Learn why traditional approaches no longer work and how to successfully move beyond them.
- **Easy application:** Achieve better and faster outcomes across a variety of situations—improving team engagement and implementation results.

SPECIALISTS

- **Better results with less aggravation:** Achieve better personal and cross-functional outcomes.
- **Easy access to ideas:** Benefit from the synthesis of more than two hundred publications and decades of experience.
- **More free time:** Get work done better and more quickly, eliminate unnecessary activities, and free up personal time.

TEACHERS, COACHES, AND CONSULTANTS

- **Shared resource:** Use *The Velocity Advantage* as a shared resource with students, employees, and coaches, capitalizing on its integration of more than fifty thousand pages from hundreds of sources and decades of business experience.

VELOCITY IS THE ULTIMATE ADVANTAGE

This book was written to help people in large organizations achieve better, faster, and more meaningful outcomes. The ideas in this book have been thoroughly tested in a variety of situations and have benefited from the input of many C-level executives, midlevel managers, and business scholars.

THIS BOOK HELPS TO TAKE SOME OF THE WORK OUT OF CROSS-FUNCTIONAL WORK

As Confucius once said, when you love what you do, you never have to work a day in your life. *The Velocity Advantage* was written to help people learn, apply, and benefit from working together in a better and more productive way. It integrates breakthrough ideas from hundreds of sources and incorporates insights from business disciplines, the social sciences, the physical sciences, technology, philosophy, and spirituality. These ideas are integrated to help people and cross-functional teams achieve better, faster, and more meaningful results in today's organizations— with less aggravation and greater engagement.

YOU ARE THIS BOOK'S ULTIMATE AUTHORITY

The Velocity Advantage incorporates ideas from some of the greatest thinkers the world has ever known, but the readers are this book's ultimate authority. No one should adopt any of the advice in this book unless it can make an immediate difference. People who are early in their careers will benefit more from some ideas, while experienced executives will benefit more from others. Marketing people will be inclined to like certain parts, finance and human resources professionals will prefer other areas, and so on. This book is designed to help a large cross section of people benefit from the same insights but, in unique ways, share a common language and approach and achieve better and faster personal and cross-functional outcomes.

What I personally bring to the table is that I have dedicated my life's work to what is in this book. I am on the board of the Drucker Institute and lead the successful and very selective firms Brand Velocity (BV) and Consequent. Earlier in my career, I had a distinguished cross-functional background in the Coca-Cola system, where I worked my way up from a front-line supervisor in a distribution center to the chief information officer (CIO) of the Coca-Cola Company's global operations. By the time I left Coke on my forty-third birthday, I had already been on the short list to become president. Since then, I have focused on helping companies adopt and benefit from the velocity advantage by creating the framework, process, and tools in this book and applying them with many large organizations across a variety of industries, including consumer products, professional services, insurance, health care, airlines, railroads, food distribution, chemicals, and manufacturing.

ORGANIZATIONS HAVE A BIG YET SOLVABLE PROBLEM

The legendary management thinker Peter Drucker first referred to the core issue that many companies need to solve as "knowledge-work productivity." This has been phrased in a much more meaningful way by Dino Robusto, the CEO of CNA Financial Corporation, as "optimizing neurons," which is the ability to create smart organizations that achieve better and faster outcomes by systematically bringing together the right knowledge, from the right people, at the right time, for the right purpose.

The Velocity Advantage focuses on doing this better and faster. This is not a natural act in large organizations and can't be achieved using traditional management approaches, which have resulted in consistent and growing dissatisfaction not only with employee engagement but also with the myriad dysfunctions that occur when smart people with unique backgrounds try to work together. Today's organizations are often very difficult places to get things done. This doesn't need to be the case. Organizations can now transcend the failures of old management practices to productively move from personal and cross-functional chaos to a more systematic way to achieve meaningful organizational outcomes.

WE CAN BE MORE SUCCESSFUL WITH LESS EFFORT

Using the Envision-Design-Build-Activate (EDBA) velocity-advantage framework described in this book is a simple and proven way to improve the speed and direction of organizational outcomes in today's companies. The approach is rooted in the social sciences because today's organizations are social enterprises. The EDBA framework and process described here provide an alternative to traditional management practices that focused on the parts instead of the whole, which worked very well in the industrial age but are completely wrong for today's organizations. Today, we need to systematically get the right knowledge integrated at the right time in dynamic environments. This book shows a better way to do this.

THE VELOCITY ADVANTAGE HAS BEEN PROVEN IN PRACTICE

The EDBA framework and process and hundreds of management insights in this book work well—and they work well together.

They can help people solve complicated issues and create organizational solutions and integrated plans in a fraction of the time these things would usually take. The difference can be amazing. Integrated corporate strategies can often be cocreated in a week using this method; they take months and cost millions of dollars using traditional approaches. Divisional strategies and action plans can often be created in a couple of days. These typically never get done the old-fashioned way. When companies apply the velocity advantage, they achieve better and faster outcomes at the project level and for their organizations overall.

SO WHAT? NOW WHAT?

In the industrial age, big companies won. Today, fast and smart companies win. If you are a "shareholder-value" person, the importance of velocity—since valuations are based on the present value of future cash flows—is an important enabler. Winning companies act with speed and direction. Slow companies eventually become yesterday's news, and their employees disengage as this occurs.

This book offers good news, because velocity increases when fewer people work fewer hours—but work differently—thus shedding the needless weight of traditional management practices. *The Velocity Advantage* helps readers successfully and systematically do this.

Foreword

Peter Drucker offered a profound caution in his now-classic book *The Effective Executive*: "The great majority of executives… are occupied with efforts rather than with results."

I remember well when Jack Bergstrand analogized for me the focus on efforts over outcomes. The roots of this focus are found in the industrial age, when productivity was mainly a function of the number of widgets produced by an assembly line in a given amount of time. The "scrap" was not an abstraction: one could literally see defective units piling up at the end of the line or coal smoke billowing out of the factory while the line sat idle. The mirror image of this challenge for today's organizations, Jack explained, is "knowledge scrap": the same waste of resources, only without any visible evidence of the problem (save, perhaps, for the grim expressions on people's faces).

Chief among the things I have learned from Jack is that the tools we use need to evolve with the work those tools are designed to manage. In our macroeconomy, the great transformation from the industrial age to the knowledge age has already taken place, yet too many organizations continue to manage by using tools developed for industrial work.

Instead, we should benefit from the implementation model described in this book, SP-AP (Strategic Profiling—Action Planning), as well as this book's integrated project-management life cycle (PMLC), to achieve more meaningful results in less time and with greater employee engagement. With SP-AP, team members learn to use and integrate their unique strengths specifically so that they can activate them to support complex, team-driven projects. SP-AP is a management tool that helps leaders and frontline workers alike stop being distracted by activity and instead focus on outcomes.

In *The Velocity Advantage*, Jack incorporates many new insights he's gained since writing his first book, *Reinvent Your Enterprise*, published in 2009. These revisions are based on what Jack and his team at Brand Velocity and Consequent have learned from using this book's ideas and tools with many executives at large corporations to markedly improve their strategies and their abilities to more rapidly solve cross-functional problems and implement organizational-transformation initiatives. They are not merely elegant theories: they have withstood the tests of the real world and are designed for the most demanding organizational circumstances.

I sympathize with the many employees who continue to use the old management tools when faced with these challenges. Although these tools are at best inadequate and often actively destructive, they are at least familiar. Jack shows us that, beyond the comfort of yesterday's practices, there is a better way.

"To try to make the future is highly risky," Drucker wrote. "It is less risky, however, than not to try to make it."

Zachary First
Executive director, Drucker Institute
Claremont Graduate University, Claremont, California

Introduction

Once upon a Time...

The principles of scientific management

FREDERICK WINSLOW TAYLOR

Today's organizations are too often filled with a lot of activity but little to show for it. Even though results typically need to come from cross-functional teams, we continue to use management techniques that were designed for factory assembly lines. In December 2015, the US Bureau of Labor Statistics reported that 80 percent of our workforce was in service-providing occupations, with less than 15 percent in goods-producing sectors; a majority of us worked with knowledge and relationships, as managerial, professional, service, sales, and office workers. Unfortunately, the management approaches that did wonders to improve manufacturing productivity in the industrial age are largely ineffective with today's people dependent interorganizational work. There is an easier and better way.

* * *

Knowledge jobs are at an all-time high, yet employee engagement hovers at an all-time low—at about 30 percent, according to Gallup. We have continued to use our tried-and-true management techniques (such as regularly scheduled meetings, strict controls, detailed plans, and extensive analyses), only to experience difficulty making organizational decisions that stick, consistently high project-failure rates, and employees whose days are filled with unproductive activities. Curiously, these issues have not stopped us from using the same management techniques that got us here. This is a little like going to a foreign country and, when we can't make ourselves understood in our native tongue, just speaking louder.

We are creatures of habit, and the hardest practices to change are those that have worked successfully in the past. In this vein, we keep trying to apply twentieth-century industrial-age management practices to collaborative work in the twenty-first century. The nature of our work changed, with success no longer coming from being bigger and by focusing on the pieces but by being faster and focusing on the big picture. Velocity (speed and direction) is one of the most important sources of internal and external success. Big, fragmented companies aren't beating small ones; fast, integrated companies are beating slow ones.

Improving results in today's organizations requires a systematic and integrated way to work together, including a common language, shared framework, repeatable process, visible stakeholder insights, productive collaboration, and integrated project management.

1. **Common language:** We live in a world filled with acronyms and specialized knowledge bases. Imagine if team members had a simple common language for working together.
2. **Shared framework:** People are wired to solve problems in significantly different ways, which continually puts

individuals and teams at cross purposes. By using a shared framework to get work done, individuals and teams can achieve better and faster outcomes in continuously changing environments.

3. **Repeatable process:** It turns out that there is a correct sequence for cross-functional work to be successfully implemented. Understanding and applying this sequence has proven to increase speed and reduce wasted effort.

4. **Stakeholder insights:** Much of today's work happens in people's heads and is invisible to others. Having visibility into how people are wired helps individuals and teams take full advantage of strengths and overcome blind spots.

5. **Productive collaboration:** Traditional collaboration is often filled with wasted effort—with a lot of activity and a few good feelings but with unsustainable outcomes. The collaborative process described in this book helps teams solve issues and develop integrated plans better and faster.

6. **Integrated project management:** Project management is very disconnected in most organizations, causing failure rates of up to 70 percent. Organizationally integrating project management helps companies move beyond this.

I personally became interested in how to systematically improve cross-functional outcomes after being routinely aggravated during transformation initiatives at large companies. At the same time, I experienced situations where people achieved work with great speed, quality, and fun. This led me to focus my professional life on helping teams and organizations move from the former to the latter.

There is a better way. Companies can serve customers better, create better organizations, and improve the speed and quality of important initiatives. Implementing projects more productively is essential because project success has a direct impact on the velocity of companies over time. According to the Project Management Institute, by 2020, the world will have more than forty million project-management jobs, of which nearly sixteen million will be new. More than $6.6 trillion—nearly 10 percent of the world's GDP—is invested in projects.

INTEGRATION PRODUCES BETTER RESULTS

Peter Drucker's work influenced me in a profound way. One of his greatest achievements was to turn management into an integrated body of knowledge. While people had written books on individual aspects of running a business, like accounting or manufacturing, no one had integrated these efforts into a holistic practice until he came on the scene.

Drucker pioneered many important management ideas, including decentralization and viewing workers as assets rather than costs. He believed that companies needed to earn the trust of their workers and were not simply profit-making machines. He was also the first to teach that the purpose of a business was to create a customer, significantly increasing the emphasis that companies placed on marketing and customer service.

He was a leadership pioneer who emphasized outcomes over charisma. Drucker saw charisma as the undoing of leaders, since it made them narcissistic and unable to change. Peter also contributed to the fields of innovation and entrepreneurship, helping organizations exploit change as an opportunity. He believed that companies were organs of society and had a responsibility to create long-term value. He was strongly against making short-term decisions that impaired a company's long-term wealth-producing capability; he also believed that short-term results were required. Simply stated, Peter Drucker was a management giant for his time and all time.

VELOCITY IS THE SECRET SAUCE

We need to work smarter, not harder; together, not separately. Where efficiency is about doing things right and effectiveness is about doing the right things, velocity improves when we do the right things in the right order in the right way.

Scientific management focused on visible, stand-alone, and repeatable factory work. Today's work is invisible, interdependent, and ever changing. It is human, not mechanical. The need to apply the social sciences to improve velocity is consistent with Sir Winston Churchill's observation that "To improve is to change and to be perfect is to change often." We need to continuously, yet cross-functionally and systematically, change how we work and how we work together.

Systematically increasing velocity in our companies also has significant social implications. For more than a century, industrial-age productivity improvements funded the economic prosperity of the developed world. By producing goods and services with less effort, more people were able to enjoy a higher standard of living. This benefited consumers and producers alike.

Healthy productivity does not exploit or oppress. It generates economic surpluses that can be used to increase wages, profits, and tax revenues. If productivity goes down, then even flat wages will not be affordable for long. If productivity went up 100 percent, wages could go up dramatically and continue to be very affordable. When companies can't increase velocity, they have to focus on the cost-oriented nature of efficiency instead of the wealth-generating nature of productivity. We cannot save our way to prosperity.

Working longer hours isn't the solution. People have become more active without becoming more productive. The result has been low employee engagement and established companies struggling to compete. Drucker warned that this would happen if we couldn't improve productivity in the knowledge economy.

Manufacturing achieved a fifty-fold productivity increase in the twentieth century. Our trajectory for knowledge-based work is pathetic by comparison.

THE VELOCITY ADVANTAGE IS SOCIO-SYSTEMATIC

Bad systems produce bad behaviors, good ones result in good behaviors, and similar systems produce the same results. To increase our potential, we need to systematically move beyond the scientific-management techniques that were designed for the industrial age and use the social sciences to achieve better and faster cross-functional outcomes.

Knowledge is a resource that can be used and kept at the same time, making it possible to achieve the greatest productivity levels the world has ever seen. At the same time, knowledge has a short shelf life, and velocity matters greatly. Systematically increasing the velocity of people's knowledge is the best way for companies to become more effective, identify and realize their potential, and create different organizations for a different future.

If we can improve the productivity of today's organizations even by a fraction of how our predecessors increased industrial productivity, we will significantly change the trajectory of our results. Employee engagement, corporate performance, and society overall will all improve as a result.

Highlights from "Once upon a Time..."

We're working too hard for the results we're getting in today's organizations. Aggravation and activity levels are too high, and employee engagement and organizational outcomes are too low.

Factory-centric scientific management, which worked well in the industrial age, is being misapplied to today's companies; this makes work difficult and unproductive.

Productivity focuses on surpluses, not costs. We have the opportunity to be uniquely productive today, because knowledge can simultaneously be used and kept (but it has a short shelf life).

Companies need to improve how they achieve organizational outcomes. Management needs to be more socio-systematic and focus on continually increasing velocity.

A 5,000 percent labor productivity improvement funded the developed world during the industrial age. We now need to improve the productivity of today's knowledge companies.

1

We Are Shackled to the Past

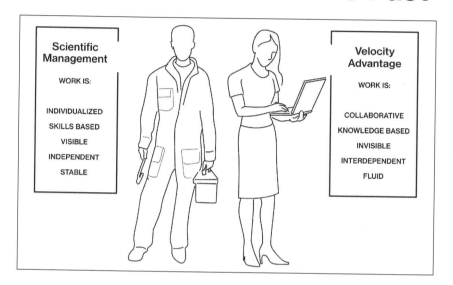

Scientific Management		Velocity Advantage
WORK IS:		WORK IS:
INDIVIDUALIZED		COLLABORATIVE
SKILLS BASED		KNOWLEDGE BASED
VISIBLE		INVISIBLE
INDEPENDENT		INTERDEPENDENT
STABLE		FLUID

We've been taught to manage interdisciplinary work in organizations the way we manage assembly lines in factories; as a result, employee disengagement and large enterprises' project-failure rates are both at about 70 percent. Trying to manage the fluid and holistic nature of cross-functional teams like factories doesn't work. It produces too many organizational silos, excessive analyses and meetings, and consistently slow and unsatisfactory outcomes. Our calendars control us, we struggle to make decisions that stick, and we become servants of our tools and metrics. In an effort to make decisions based on facts, we are drowning in our own data. We struggle to make cross-functional decisions and implement them once they are made. Factory-based scientific management is consistently failing us.

*   *   *

We compete in a world that is very fluid, as fluid as knowledge itself. Our work is ever changing and often ambiguous, yet we continue to manage like we did during the Industrial Revolution—with highly detailed and preplanned work, managers who try to do the thinking for the workers, workers who expect to be told what to do, and strong functional and organizational divisions. The work has changed, but how it is managed has not adapted. We simply use more advanced and expensive tools, often doing excellently what shouldn't be done at all. Factory-based scientific management lives on because it is the devil we know. Even though we live in a world of constant change, companies continue to cling to practices that were designed for the predictable and repeatable nature of assembly lines and blue-collar work processes.

When I first read Drucker's book *Post-Capitalist Society*, it changed the course of my professional life. In a similar way to the fish that doesn't recognize that it's in water, I hadn't thought very deeply about the nature of my own work environment. Yet I was *very* aware of its by-products: crazy schedules, slow decision making, weak engagement, contentious relationships, PowerPoints preferred over actual outcomes, and inconsistent execution.

Companies and business schools have clung to scientific-management-based practices because they worked so well in the past and because there is often great comfort in being a specialist without having a responsibility for making these specialties effective in cross-functional environments. The nature of today's knowledge organizations is very different from that of industrialized factories. With physical work, people who are carpenters and assembly-line workers work hard for a living. When they finish the day, it is visibly clear to them and to others what they have accomplished. In modern companies, people who are researchers, subject-matter experts, analysts, and managers also work hard for a living. Yet at the end of each day, their achievements are not always as clear. People can work on something that was urgent in the morning but is no longer important by dinnertime. With physical work, we can visibly see the waste that comes from not working (or from working on the wrong things). When people work with their knowledge, this waste is often invisible. It is costly nonetheless.

Working with knowledge, and especially cross-functional knowledge, can be extremely productive because an idea can be used and kept at the same time. It is unproductive, however, to manage it using approaches that were designed for industrial work. Knowledge is invisible; it happens inside our heads. Activities expand to fill the time available, resources often calcify around previous priorities through historically based budgets, and workers commonly rise to their levels of incompetence. Similar to the old advertising adage, half a company's knowledge is wasted—we just don't know which half.

Information technology (IT), as sophisticated as it has become since the industrial age, often does not address this problem. The greatest complaint I hear from non-IT executives is how slow their IT progress is. I also hear great dissatisfaction from IT organizations about how difficult it is to partner with business leaders. Many years ago, the Nobel laureate and economist Robert Solow called this same problem the *productivity paradox* after he found that large investments in IT contributed very little to the productivity improvement of established companies. In today's digital age, this continues to be true in many organizations. In the time since Solow wrote that "you can find the computer age everywhere but in the productivity statistics," the advancement of IT has exceeded most people's wildest expectations. Yet, most established companies struggle with getting good returns on these investments; for example, major enterprise initiatives suffer 70 percent project-failure rates and legacy systems are almost always very difficult to replace.

The productivity of cross-functional work has continually struggled while the sophistication of technology has skyrocketed. Yet one depends on the other, and established companies often fail to capitalize on the potential of rapidly advancing technologies. Investment and effort are not in short supply (nor are consulting firms and technology companies selling their wares), but the game-changing outcomes have been and continue to be few and far between in large organizations. Companies can easily point to activities, but they struggle to achieve successful outcomes. They are often unable to replace their legacy systems, develop consistent information architectures, and productively govern even the most basic cross-functional technology initiatives. The problem is not technology. It's the lack of cross-functional velocity. In the decades since Solow's discovery, the fruits of technological progress have usually grown on the trees of new entrants—in my lifetime companies like Apple, Google, Microsoft, Amazon, Facebook, Tesla, Uber, and Airbnb.

Established companies have the remarkable opportunity to leapfrog the productivity paradox by systematically and cross-functionally solving critical problems and capitalizing on important opportunities.

In today's companies, velocity needs to be judged by the speed and quality of outcomes, not by the amount of energy expended. Important organizational outcomes include:

- Something that isn't producing results is stopped.
- An island of strength has been improved or expanded.
- Something new is successfully up and running.

We can do a much better job of achieving better performance *from* and building more fun *into* our companies by improving the velocity of our individual and cross-functional efforts. But we need to work differently for this to happen.

SCIENTIFIC MANAGEMENT WAS PERFECT FOR ITS TIME

Frederick Taylor, the father of the scientific-management movement, used standard processes and the division of labor to improve labor productivity and to institutionalize the practice of piecework in factories. Because the nature of the work was stable, he was able to achieve great things by focusing on the parts, because the whole was obvious.

Taylor dramatically improved labor productivity in the industrial age. He simplified repeatable jobs so that workers could efficiently perform their activities. He also introduced objective processes and measures, including the practice of formally allocating time for managers to plan the work of their employees. This management approach was as repeatable as the work itself. It continues to work well with the visible, independent, stable, and repeatable nature of industrial work. It's not effective with the invisible, interdependent, and dynamic nature of modern organizations. Organizations don't work like factories, and when Taylor's methods are applied to cross-functional projects, they too often get overengineered and have difficulties adapting in a changing environment.

IT'S NOW TIME TO MOVE BEYOND TAYLORISM

MBA programs continue to emphasize the quantitative side of management. Managing organizational outcomes, however, requires that we use situational knowledge in dynamic environments. In a factory, just as in a spreadsheet, the same input will always produce the same output. In today's organizations, the same input will commonly produce a different output—influenced by the particular people and circumstances involved.

To win in the knowledge age, companies need to productively integrate and activate organizational visions, expertise, processes, and relationships. Today's work is relational, project oriented, and interdependent. It requires an ability to rapidly apply knowledge to new situations and to identify and solve bottlenecks, since a delay in one area can keep the whole from moving forward. Spending time on something that does not produce successful outcomes is no different from producing scrap on a factory floor. Given the rapid half-life of knowledge, good ideas do not stay good for long. This is one reason why velocity is so important.

Although cross-functional initiatives should not be managed like factories, they *do* need to be systematically implemented, because they can go awry in a variety of ways—for example,

- not having the right people involved at the right time;
- too many meetings that produce too few actions;
- competing internal priorities that have no resolution;
- executing studies that are completed and put on the shelf;
- implementing projects unproductively; and
- high executive turnover, causing changes in direction.

It's beneficial to manage cross-functional work differently because of the tendency for it to expand to fill the available time and because of the disconnects that naturally occur within and across departmental lines. To improve velocity, we need to manage socio-systematically—with clarity about who is in charge and at what time, for what reason, and for how long.

Cross-functional work benefits from the collaboration of people with specific knowledge and defined organizational authority in a way that incorporates the social sciences.

CROSS-FUNCTIONAL INITIATIVES FUEL THE VELOCITY ADVANTAGE

Cross-functional initiatives are similar to factory work in that the goal of both is to generate surpluses. Since today's work is knowledge based, while the potential surplus is larger, the shelf

Frederick Taylor	Peter Drucker	Velocity Advantage
Define tasks	Understand tasks	Cocreate tasks
Command and control	Give autonomy	Collaborate and integrate
Strict standards	Continuous innovation	Achieve better and faster outcomes
Focus on quantity	Focus on quality	Focus on the right things in the right order
Measure work to a strict standard	Continuously learn and teach	Learn and teach through facilitated collaboration
Minimize the cost of workers for a task	Treat workers as an asset, not a cost	Engage the right people at the right time to produce the best outcomes

life is shorter. These two countervailing forces make velocity an essential ingredient for success.

Knowledge does not have the constraints that physical labor does. For example, think of dog walkers in New York City. In the tradition of Frederick Taylor, they increase their surplus by walking many dogs at the same time. Their productivity increases proportionally to the number of dogs they can handle. Meanwhile, in Omaha, Nebraska, there is Warren Buffett—one of the richest people on earth. As an investor, he has earned large financial surpluses and required very few people to do it.

Physical work has physical limits. People can walk a lot of dogs, but they do have constraints. Applying knowledge can be much more productive. In Buffett's case, investing a little or a lot—given a similar level of expertise—requires roughly the same amount of work. Buffett's firm, Berkshire Hathaway, earned a net income of $24 billion in 2016 with a staff of twenty-five people.

Most companies will never be as productive as Berkshire Hathaway, but the point is that knowledge is almost infinitely scalable—and most companies can do a better job of managing it. The velocity advantage can help people and their organizations capitalize on this.

Taylor	Drucker	Velocity Advantage
Work is visible	Work is invisible	Systematically manages invisible work to produce visible outcomes
Work focuses on the parts	Work focuses on the whole	Incorporates a specific yet holistic process
Work is predictable	Work requires continuity and change	Capitalizes on cocreation and integration: EDBA
Emphasizes running things	Emphasizes changing things	Emphasizes achieving outcomes
More structure with fewer decisions	Less structure with more decisions	A consistent structure for more productive decisions
Focus on the right answers	Focus on the right questions	Focus on the right people, framework, and process

Productivity in factories increased with the clear division of labor and the use of fixed assembly lines. Cross-functional work benefits from more of a sociological approach, including a shared language, framework, and process; visible stakeholder insights; facilitated collaboration; and integrated project management. It is not only what people know that matters but also how fast that knowledge can be integrated and applied—both inside the organization and in the marketplace.

NEURONS ARE OUR UNITS OF PRODUCTION

Achieving outcomes in today's companies is a social process. Numbers are important, but improving velocity does not begin with analysis. This is not a new idea. The sociologist Daniel Bell researched the structural changes leading to the information age in the early 1970s, making a clear distinction between information and knowledge. People often talk about information and knowledge interchangeably, but there is an important difference: knowledge is alive, whereas information is not. As soon as knowledge becomes information, it is no longer knowledge.

In organizations, the difference between information and knowledge is a little like the difference between a mounted deer and the living deer that it once was. While a deer that comes from a taxidermist resembles a living deer, it cannot respond to change. Information can only adapt as knowledge adapts. This is even true in our current world of big data, business analytics, and digitization. Even in a world dominated by machine learning, the velocity advantage is important to improving organizational outcomes—perhaps even more important. What can be done with information and systems is impressive, but knowledge is a human output, with individual and collective creativity, organizational influence, personal power, negotiation abilities, ambition, and intuition. If the source is not breathing, the output is not knowledge.

Since knowledge is our most important factor of production, and since the half-life of knowledge is short, we need to systematically increase velocity in order to learn faster, interact better, and produce better and faster cross-functional results. The next chapter shows how to do this.

Highlights from "We Are Shackled to the Past"

Today, work is often aggravating and unproductive, with crazy schedules, slow decision making, weak engagement and teamwork, and inconsistent execution quality.

Traditional scientific management was designed for the visible, subdivided, and unchanging nature of physical work. The nature of organizations is very different.

Knowledge can be hyperproductive because ideas can simultaneously be used and kept. But since knowledge has a short shelf life, velocity (speed and direction) is critical.

Knowledge is alive, whereas information is not. Improving velocity doesn't require better information but a more systematic social process to achieve better and faster outcomes.

Managing today's work needs to move beyond Taylor, build upon Drucker, and use a socio-systematic approach that goes beyond both.

2

Velocity Is Socio-Systematic

" Social Science...
It's less complex
and more
complicated than
normal science "

To win in our rapidly changing marketplace and organizations, we
need to stop trying to treat organizations like machines and instead
organize people and integrate their knowledge in a way that achieves
better and faster outcomes. To do this, a minor amount of *complexity*—
in the form of a shared framework, language, and process—up front
helps to avoid an unworkable amount of organizational *complication*
over time. Chess grand masters do something conceptually similar by
viewing chessboards in large chunks, whereas amateurs focus on iso-
lated moves. Less skilled players struggle with a far greater amount of
complication because they don't incorporate enough strategic complexity—making it difficult for them to win. In chess and organizations
alike, this lack of a holistic approach undermines successful outcomes.

*   *   *

We can achieve better and faster outcomes by working in a way that is rooted in the social sciences; managing physical work, which is the "sweet spot" of scientific management, is easy by comparison. It is relatively easy to see what is happening on a production line from beginning to end. When a problem happens on the factory floor, where that problem is occurring and why is very visible. Managing work through people in organizations is not nearly as straightforward.

By managing differently, cross-functional teams can help organizations be better, faster, and more successful. In organizations, our work has many interdependent and continually evolving parts, and improving one piece does not necessarily improve the whole. For example, if marketing is not the constraint in a company, then focusing more on marketing will not improve the firm's overall performance. On the contrary, it could weaken it by misallocating resources.

In cross-functional initiatives, the equivalent of an assembly line is a shared framework, language, and process; insights about key stakeholders; strategic collaboration; and organizationally integrated project management. To solve problems and capitalize on opportunities, cross-functional teams need to be on the same page, move in a single direction, have a way to adapt in an ever-changing environment, and implement projects in an integrated way.

Without an integrated approach, it is very easy for teams to run into problems. Stakeholders have differing backgrounds, objectives, personalities, ways of solving problems, and so on.

When I was on the board of Nordic Beverages, a joint venture between the Coca-Cola Company and Carlsberg, we discussed the implementation of a large software initiative in Carlsberg's Copenhagen headquarters. One of the board members was rightly focused on asking *what* the project was going to achieve.

Another concentrated on *who* was going to be responsible for what. A third member focused on *how* the project was going to be done. For a couple of hours, the company's CEO and CIO fielded a series of questions and follow-up questions and listened to a few personal philosophies and life experiences along the way.

One of the board members put it all together and asked *where* they saw the project going, *why*, and *over what time frame; what* the key priorities were and *when* they would be completed; *how* the priorities could best be achieved; and *who* was going to be responsible for what. It was a challenge for management to answer these questions, as a team, in an integrated way. This is commonly the case when people don't use an integrated approach. Nonetheless, getting these *where, why, what, when, how,* and *who* questions wrong, or in the wrong order, costs companies dearly.

Stakeholders need a shared way to get on the same page and work in a single *where, why, what, when, how,* and *who* direction. People sometimes *are* clear on this at an individual level but, due to differing views, are not synchronized as a group. The group view is what matters most with cross-functional work. The absence of an integrated approach decreases the velocity of many important company-wide initiatives and companies overall— resulting in wasted resources, reduced employee engagement, and high project-failure rates.

ORGANIZATIONS ARE NOT ASSEMBLY LINES

Where scientific management is based on the objective and mechanized work methods developed by Taylor, today's work requires a combination of subjective *and* objective steps implemented in the right order. When we try to scientifically manage today's work, it gets overengineered—taking longer, producing more rework as environments change, and costing more to achieve desired outcomes. Work that would otherwise benefit from a just-in-time approach gets slowed down from overly detailed "just in case" analyses. Some of the symptoms of continually trying to manage organizations like assembly lines include an inability for workers to see the forest for the trees, resources spent on overly detailed analysis and too much planning up front before it is clear what the destination and priorities are, and the lack of a strategic compass to help teams productively adjust to changing conditions.

With industrialized work, investing more in detailed analysis improves results and reduces risks, such as when designing or building a bridge or skyscraper. With the dynamic nature of cross-functional work, systematically taking a just-in-time approach is often more productive and less risky—guided by a stable vision for success combined with continuous and rapid improvements.

Where factories benefit from specialization, organizational outcomes improve with a more holistic and people-centered approach. As with the chess grand masters described earlier in the chapter, a minor amount of complexity on the front end helps to avoid an unworkable amount of complication later.

The terms *complexity* and *complication* are often used interchangeably, but they are different when it comes to achieving better and faster organizational outcomes. Complex systems have a coherent architecture, as with a computer chip. There can be many pathways, but the same inputs will always result in the same outputs. People are not complex; we are complicated. The same inputs can produce different outputs in varying situations. Large organizations and projects regularly struggle—not because they are complex, but because they are complicated. Scientific management cannot deal with this, but the social sciences can.

Unlike complex computer chips or assembly lines, organizations are complicated due to human inconsistencies and the invisible nature of what is going on in people's heads. On one hand, human organizations are constrained because most people can only concentrate effectively on a few things at a time. Yet, since human intelligence and creativity are unbounded, teams and organizations can be uniquely powerful. Due to the underlying differences between complication and complexity, cross-functional teams perform best through a socio-systematic approach.

THE SOCIAL SCIENCES ARE BUILT INTO THE EDBA PROCESS

The velocity-advantage approach is a proven way to help people achieve better and faster outcomes, with less aggravation, by systematically applying the social sciences to cross-functional work. The method helps organizations integrate otherwise conflicting mental models, cocreate better solutions, and implement priorities more productively.

The EDBA framework and process described in this book are heavily influenced by the social sciences, including research from Gibson Burrell and Gareth Morgan. Burrell and Morgan published a seminal book on the history of sociological paradigms, classifying a comprehensive set of sociological studies into four groups using the four poles of subjectivity, objectivity, stability, and change. The sociological paradigm outputs of Intuition, Analysis, Process, and Emotion, helped guide the Envision-Design-Build-Activate model:

- **Intuition**—Envision
- **Analysis**—Design
- **Process**—Build
- **Emotion**—Activate

Burrell and Morgan labeled their sociological orientations interpretive, functionalist, radical structuralist, and radical humanist. Their work was groundbreaking for its intended purpose of categorizing a large number of sociological paradigms into a unified framework. A side benefit for me was that it provided a

way to begin to conceptualize a better way to manage knowl-
edge- and relationship-based initiatives in large organizations.
Organizations are social constructions, and applying knowledge
to issues and opportunities is a social process. Even though there
is no single model to integrate the social sciences, Burrell and
Morgan's framework was a good starting point.

Although four-quadrant models such as EDBA are frequently
used in business and in the social sciences alike, there is a difference in how models are conceptualized. In business, consultants
often compare two variables to create four-quadrant models.
One difference between the two-by-two matrices used in business and the four-quadrant models used in the social sciences
is that social-science models are more likely to unite two sets of
competing ideas, producing frameworks that are more holistic.
The Burrell and Morgan model does not compare stability versus
change or objectivity versus subjectivity; it views both at the same
time and accommodates many variations in between.

Embracing opposites helps when managing organizational
activities, because many opposing forces are often going on at
the same time. In business, the integration of opposites occurs
regularly. An objective approach works well in accounting, but
a subjective approach will often work better in sales. Neither is
inherently good nor bad; the most productive approach depends
upon the subject, situation, and person.

Carl Jung, the Swiss psychiatrist who inspired the Myers-
Briggs Type Indicator, also embraced opposites. He focused on
thinking *and* feeling and incorporated dominant and secondary
orientations for these characteristics, with one working in the
background and the other in command, depending on the situation. The author Ned Herrmann, creator of the Herrmann Brain
Dominance Instrument, saw something similar when he worked
at General Electric. Like Jung, he found that different orientations were either less or more effective in different situations.

The EDBA velocity-advantage framework focuses on the four poles of knowledge, work, subjectivity, and objectivity. These poles produce four orientations that are simultaneously distinct, integrated, and able to be sequenced:

- **Step one:** subjective knowledge—**Envision**
- **Step two:** objective knowledge—**Design**
- **Step three:** objective work—**Build**
- **Step four:** subjective work—**Activate**

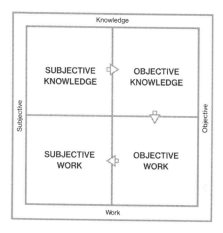

Applying the velocity-advantage model—in conjunction with integrated cross-functional facilitation and project management—helps cross-functional teams live and work in two worlds: the world of ideas and knowledge and the world of people and work. The model is logically consistent with the four Burrell and Morgan orientations (intuition, analysis, process, and emotional). Relating this model to the Nordic Beverages board of directors example mentioned at the beginning of this chapter, the Envision step helps establish a shared view of *where* you intend to go and *why* (for a given time frame). The

Design step then helps prioritize *what* you need to do and *when*. Through the Build step, people then determine *how* to best implement the design priorities. Through the Activate step, stakeholders choose *who* will be the best to implement the Build tasks. Once the cycle is completed, the outcome is produced. Getting good at applying this systematically increases velocity.

VELOCITY CAN BE SYSTEMATICALLY INCREASED

EDBA is a proven way to collaboratively organize the opposing forces of knowledge, work, subjectivity, and objectivity.

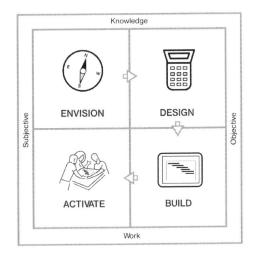

Through Envision, people cocreate the destination and time frame. Once Envision is clear, Design establishes the most important priorities required to implement it. The third step is Build, which focuses on how to most productively implement the priorities. Then, through Activate, the right people are assigned to the right work at the right time. Through these four steps, human knowledge is converted into organizational outcomes.

ENVISION – WHERE AND WHY

Strong Envision-oriented people get energy from subjective knowledge and are instinctively wired to determine *where to go and why* for a given time frame.

- In companies, Envision-oriented functions include research and development, strategy, marketing, and other externally influenced functions such as public affairs.
- Envision-oriented people have an innate ability to think outside the box. A weakness is that they can be impractical when it comes to what is most important at the moment.
- Envision characteristics include the following:
  —thinking strategically
  —creating a visionary destination
  —thinking inventively
  —generating new ideas
  —being creative
  —seeing the big picture
  —brainstorming new ideas

DESIGN – WHAT AND WHEN

Armed with a clear Envision statement, strong Design-oriented people are able to objectively establish *what* priorities are needed *when*.

- In companies, Design-oriented functions include finance, accounting, engineering, and planning.
- Design-oriented people are great with plans, numbers, and measures. A weakness is that they can be inflexible and not see the forest for the trees during changing environments.

19

- Design characteristics include the following:
  —analyzing situations
  —establishing clear rules
  —establishing detailed objectives
  —planning details
  —establishing clear measures
  —being objective
  —making decisions by the numbers

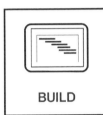

BUILD

BUILD – HOW

Strong Build-oriented people are great at determining *how the priorities established in Design can best get done.* They are very good at organizing and implementing work processes. Build-oriented company functions include areas such as manufacturing, information systems, and logistics.

- Build-oriented people are practical, precise, and good at turning priorities into repeatable processes. A weakness is that they are inclined to stubbornly defend the status quo.
- Build characteristics include the following:
  —following standard processes
  —implementing step-by-step procedures
  —implementing complex projects
  —integrating systems
  —using proven methods
  —implementing solutions to problems
  —implementing clear roles and responsibilities

ACTIVATE

ACTIVATE – WHO

Strong Activate-oriented people are great at the *who* factor—they are able to motivate team members and achieve results through others.

- In companies, Activate-oriented functions include areas such as line management, coaching, communications, and sales.
- Activate-oriented people are great at solving problems through personal relationships and influence. A weakness is that it can be difficult for them to be consistent and follow established rules.
- Activate characteristics include the following:
  —building strong personal relationships
  —working in teams
  —coaching others
  —emotionally supporting others
  —relating to people
  —communicating
  —being spontaneous

The EDBA approach helps companies in a variety of situations to get interdisciplinary work completed better and faster. It is well tested and integrates decades of experience and insights from some of the world's best thought leaders.

The sequence of the steps—moving from Envision to Design, Design to Build, and Build to Activate—has been proven in practice and is influenced by Norbert Wiener and Talcott Parsons's work on social cybernetics (the science of relationships, control, and organization). Wiener, a mathematician, first used cybernetics in 1948 to facilitate self-steering, which is how radar is used to help steer airplanes. By using information generated by radar, a plane's flight path can be automated to stay on course.

In 1951, Parsons, a sociologist, applied Wiener's cybernetics work to social systems through his general theory of action. He created what he termed the *cybernetic hierarchy* to try to improve the effect of organizational actions. The cybernetic hierarchy is consistent with the EDBA sequence. Like the theory of action, Envision helps teams adapt to the external environment. This results in priorities that are Designed and helps to Build integrated systems that are implemented by motivated Activators. Looked at through a sociological lens, the EDBA process operationalizes Parsons's cybernetic hierarchy to help organizations increase the velocity of important outcomes on a systematic basis and in a practical way.

EDBA IS AN UNCHANGING WAY TO CONTINUOUSLY CHANGE

After applying the EDBA model and process thousands of times, I've found that it consistently helps cross-functional teams to solve complex business issues better and faster. Integrated strategies can be completed in days, and most business issues can be solved, in a cross-functional way, in less than a day. Project charters and business requirements can be completed better and in a fraction of the time it takes using other methods. The reasons for cross-functional failures that haven't used the velocity advantage are also clear. First, there isn't a common framework and language between key constituents at the right time. Second, one or more of the EDBA steps are missing. Third, the EDBA process gets out of sequence. Finally, the EDBA action plan is not managed in an integrated and cross-functional way.

Cross-functional outcomes can be managed more holistically and successfully using the socio-systematic EDBA framework and process. As will be described later, when one part of the EDBA system changes, the rest can adjust in a holistic way by using the velocity-advantage approach. All four EDBA steps are important in and of themselves but benefit from being managed as a holistic system. Work is unproductive when the four parts of the EDBA system are disconnected or out of sequence. This is true for individuals, teams, projects, and organizations alike. Since most of us can remember only a limited number of things at any one time, the four parts of the EDBA process are akin to using a magical sociological number of variables.

Using the EDBA velocity advantage, organizations can much more rapidly and successfully capitalize on and adapt to changing environments. Once people gain experience with the velocity advantage, it becomes a natural way to apply a familiar approach to a variety of new situations. In the words of the late singer-songwriter John Denver, we can come home to a place we've never been before—to achieve better and faster results across a variety of circumstances in an ever-changing world.

VELOCITY IS OUR MOST SUSTAINABLE ADVANTAGE

While at Coke, I was interviewed for Bill Gates's book *Business @ the Speed of Thought.* In his book, he wrote that the past benefited from quality and reengineering, but the future depends on velocity. Velocity—speed and direction—is essential for today's companies. Success is not about speed *or* direction. It requires speed *and* direction.

There has never been a better time to make present businesses more effective, identify and realize their potential, and turn them into different businesses for a different future. We can achieve this by simply asking, answering, and operationalizing the four socio-systematic EDBA questions and doing so in the right order and in an integrated way:

- **Envision:** *Where* and *why* for a given time frame
- **Design:** *What* priorities *when*
- **Build:** *How* to best achieve these priorities
- **Activate:** *Who* is best to achieve each step

This may sound too simple. I wouldn't blame anyone for thinking this. But I have witnessed countless breakthroughs when companies have applied the social science-based EDBA process to cross-functional organizational problems and opportunities. Initiatives that were previously struggling have been turned around, and projects that were started using EDBA have consistently succeeded. The power of a shared framework, language, and process; well-understood stakeholder insights; facilitated collaboration; and integrated project management makes all the difference.

Highlights from "Velocity Is Socio-Systematic"
Systematically incorporating the social sciences into cross-functional work gets better results with less aggravation.
To unleash the potential of cross-functional teams, focus on answering four questions in the right order: (1) where and why for a given time frame, (2) what and when, (3) how, and (4) who?
Applying the EDBA framework and process is a proven way to successfully manage the invisible, interdependent, and continually evolving nature of today's organizational issues.
Unlike scientific management, in which the parts can be managed separately, organizations need to holistically integrate where, why, what, when, how, and who.
The velocity advantage is a proven way to improve results by helping teams convert ideas into integrated plans and then turn those plans into successful outcomes.

3

Activate Your Velocity Advantage

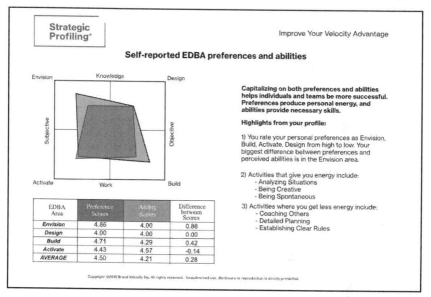

One benefit of the velocity advantage is how easy it is to get started. All it takes is a project, a cross-functional team, and a Strategic Profiling— Action Planning (SP-AP) facilitated session. These sessions usually last from four to eight hours and often eliminate weeks and even months of wasted effort in key initiatives. SP-AP helps stakeholders collaboratively apply the Envision-Design-Build-Activate (EDBA) framework, language, and process to solve complicated problems, establish key priorities, build integrated plans, and ensure that the right people are engaged at the right time. Some of the by-products are that team bonding increases, people teach and learn from one another, and downstream user-requirement misunderstandings are reduced or eliminated altogether.

*   *   *

SP-AP INCREASES VELOCITY SOCIO-SYSTEMATICALLY

Prior to SP-AP, many companies successfully used the EDBA process to help teams get the right work done in the right order by the right people. People quickly understood it and agreed with it. It was common sense that teams shouldn't work on priorities (Design) until the destination and time frame (Envision) were clear. Similarly, it didn't make sense to develop processes and systems (Build) until the priorities were clear in Design. It was also obvious that the "how" work that is done in Build should determine which people are needed in the Activate step.

Yet, prior to SP-AP, even though people embraced the EDBA process, they sometimes got stuck as cross-functional teams. Things were better, but there were still inconsistencies within and across groups when connecting the dots between the where, what, when, how, and who. This kept teams from being as fast and effective as they were capable of being, and unnecessarily increased the amount of effort required.

SP-AP was developed to address this. First, I reflected on my previous use of "personality instruments." I had taken Myers-Briggs many years before and still remembered that I was an INTJ (i.e., **I**ntroversion-i**N**tuition-**T**hinking-**J**udgment) type. While Myers-Briggs and other such instruments are insightful and memorable, they didn't connect to a cross-functional implementation process, which limited their effectiveness. The same was and is true with other surveys on the market. They are all interesting, but their ability to improve and accelerate cross-functional outcomes is limited.

Incorporating many of the benefits of personality instruments and filling in the voids, the Strategic Profiling (SP) survey was developed, which produces important individual, team, and company EDBA insights. SP quickly helps people internalize the velocity-advantage framework and understand how it relates to the success of their particular teams and projects.

Using SP with teams was an important step forward, but the survey needed to be operationalized further. By combining the SP results with facilitated cross-functional collaboration, teams were able to systematically achieve what previously wasn't possible. Through SP-AP, we found that companies could use functional experts for short periods of time to solve complicated issues. SP-AP is like a day in the life of the velocity advantage. In these sessions, key stakeholders cocreate a single destination and time frame, set priorities, determine how to best implement these priorities, and choose the best people to contribute at the most appropriate times.

With SP-AP, teams achieve better and faster outcomes while also building reusable capabilities for improving other critical initiatives. A side benefit is that people learn a tremendous amount from one another during the SP-AP process, and they buy in to the plans in a way that doesn't happen the old-fashioned way (for example, with extensive preplanning, charters, steering committees, separated project teams, and the like.) We have discovered that the time spent in SP-AP sessions is worth it for the information sharing, organizational alignment, and team building alone. But these are only side benefits. Through SP-AP, teams rapidly cocreate cross-functional solutions that are integrated and actionable. This helps turn EDBA from a conceptual framework into an organizational capability.

SP-AP is a step-by-step process in which:

1. A sponsor identifies a key problem or opportunity.
2. The best people are chosen to work on it for a few hours.
3. Participants take the twenty-minute SP survey.

4. The SP data is analyzed for the individuals and teams.
5. People rapidly cocreate integrated solutions.
6. Integrated EDBA action plans are developed.
7. The next steps begin immediately.

SP-AP outcomes are integrated, which:

- establishes a common language and process;
- provides many individual and organizational insights;
- improves personal development and team alignment;
- produces the best and most actionable solutions possible;
- results in an integrated action plan for moving forward.

Velocity increases through applying SP-AP, which:

- improves cross-functional strategies;
- helps when new leaders arrive;
- improves key initiatives;
- helps set functional and cross-functional priorities;
- rapidly addresses important issues and opportunties.

Improves cross-functional strategies

After A. G. Lafley and Roger Martin wrote the book *Playing to Win*, I had the opportunity to meet with them both. The superiority of their strategy approach from a cross-functional perspective was immediately compelling. Our BV and Consequent consultants have often worked with clients in *Playing to Win* strategy sessions, starting with SP-AP. Doing this has helped leaders activate and integrate their knowledge to more rapidly address specific strategic problems and strategic choices. It also helps key stakeholders jointly connect the dots between strategic choices and the ability to operationalize them. The learning, teaching, and strategic breakthroughs that happen in these sessions are remarkable. On a particular divisional strategy, the CFO of a large company said he learned more about that line of business in a couple of days than he had learned in the last three and a half years. Whether the strategy is used for companies, functions, or business ecosystems, *Playing to Win* with SP-AP can dramatically improve an organization's strategic process.

Helps when new leaders arrive

There is often a lot of wasted time, frustration, and even fear when new leaders join organizations. This also occurs when key people join established teams or when new teams are formed. These changes often begin with conflicting—and often invisible—expectations, unclear priorities, conflicting mental models, and unfamiliar terminology.

SP-AP dramatically improves the learning curve for the leader, and for the team relative to their new boss, when new people are put in place. SP-AP can also help firms determine the degree of fit between the individual needed and the situational needs of the employing company for specific positions. Incorporating SP-AP increases velocity from the beginning and throughout the person's assignment.

Improves key initiatives

Team-building events are often fun and sometimes useful. Unfortunately, the time spent on team building is often not connected to immediate business issues, and the good feelings produced fade by the time tough business matters need to be addressed. SP-AP improves teamwork and team results as a natural by-product of helping groups collaborate on and problem solve important issues using the velocity-advantage process. By learning and applying EDBA, teams implement better and more integrated solutions better and faster. By using the EDBA project-management life cycle (PMLC), stakeholders can further improve the velocity of their implementation efforts. Project managers can take full advantage of subject-matter experts; using this approach to allow key people to concentrate more on their day-to-day jobs.

Helps set functional and cross-functional priorities

An easy way to tell if organizations are unproductive is to see if schedules are crammed, meetings are out of control, and the to-do list has significantly more projects on it than can possibly be executed. This happens when organizations are managed in a piecemeal way, making it difficult to set clear priorities on a company-wide level. SP-AP sessions help address this. By getting the right people together in a facilitated SP-AP session, leaders set priorities more holistically and productively. The clear priorities can then be staffed and funded appropriately and executed in an integrated way; people can also increase clarity about which ideas are not priorities. This helps companies systematically improve velocity at both the project and organizational levels.

Rapidly addresses important issues and opportunities

SP-AP helps cross-functional teams rapidly integrate and apply their knowledge to important priorities. This helps get the experts *and* project teams off to a good start. Then, over the course of the projects, SP-AP helps companies manage the transitions between phases, when different people are needed to productively build upon the work that has already been done. Using traditional methods, projects often get off to a fast start and then get bogged down due to insufficient integration. Alternatively, they start too slowly, with planning that is too detailed and governance structures that are too complicated. By incorporating SP-AP into key initiatives, cross-functional teams first focus on the right things and then do them right—taking full advantage of the knowledge of the primary stakeholders and project team members.

A key advantage is that SP-AP is socio-systematic

SP-AP systematically applies the social sciences to improve cross-functional outcomes. It helps teams understand and apply key EDBA insights to integrate their best ideas faster and save time and money when implementing key initiatives. SP-AP also helps participants achieve more success in their organizations by developing better relationships with key stakeholders. SP-AP is effective with teams of less than ten and groups of hundreds of people.

Where traditional, scientifically-based management focuses on the parts, SP-AP helps organizations manage the whole. It uses the EDBA framework and incorporates a number of important business, psychological, and sociological insights into the process. The Strategic Profiling survey maps people's preferences and abilities to the EDBA framework, with fifteen different Strategic Profiles possible. The personal version of SP has thirty-five questions, while the team version has sixty-five. Every Strategic Profile provides a unique productivity path.

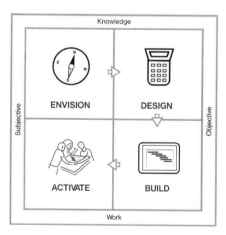

Borrowing from science fiction to provide an illustration, if the four main *Star Trek* characters took SP, they would have all four EDBA areas covered: the visionary Captain Kirk (Envision), the logical Mr. Spock (Design), the ship's engineer Scotty (Build), and the medical officer Dr. "Bones" McCoy (Activate). Similar to business organizations, people like Mr. Spock and Scotty, with their objective natures, are often perplexed by the intuitive subjectivity of people like Captain Kirk. People like Bones and Spock are also commonly at odds when logic and emotions clash. In companies, these clashes happen when innovators (Envision), accountants (Design), manufacturing people (Build), and sales professionals (Activate) work together. Just as every EDBA type helps *Star Trek*'s USS *Enterprise*, they are also needed (but need to work together systematically) to help today's business enterprises.

SP helps make the invisible visible

SP helps individuals and teams understand and leverage their EDBA-related preferences and abilities. The survey is not a test, nor is it intended to label folks. Its purpose is to help teams internalize EDBA and to use that knowledge to cocreate and implement solutions better and faster. If someone does not agree with his or her SP results (which is rarely the case, as it turns out), that's OK. It's best to not get hung up on the profiles. SP provides many insights, but the main purpose is to help people understand and apply the EDBA model to produce better and faster cross-functional outcomes.

With SP survey results, if someone has a strong ability and preference in the same EDBA area, then this is probably their sweet spot. On the other hand, it can mean a couple of different things if someone's ability is in one area and his or her preference is in another. If people have a strong ability in Build and a strong preference in Envision, they might have unique insights on the visionary use of systems and processes. But in the future, they might benefit from Envision-related assignments—where they will get more energy and personal satisfaction.

EDBA preferences versus perceived abilities are most important with executives, because they often have other people in their organizations who can help them with their nonpreferences. Gaps identify potential blind spots. Regardless of someone's preferences, all the EDBA steps are necessary and need to be completed in the right order. While it is fine for executives to delegate to others, abdicating personal accountability—and not ensuring that all four EDBA areas are connected—is asking for trouble.

THE EDBA SEQUENCE PRODUCES THE VELOCITY ADVANTAGE

Every Strategic Profile provides a unique productivity path. The more holistic the profile, the more important it is to get the EDBA sequence right (i.e., Envision in front of Design, Design in front of Build, and Build in front of Activate). This is especially important with cross-functional teams, because groups often have holistic profiles (which is one reason they get stuck so frequently). If the Strategic Profile is holistic, the name of the game is sequence. If the profile is skewed, the key is to fill in the EDBA gaps. (But sequence is still essential.)

SP identifies productivity paths to increase velocity for individuals and teams. For example, with Strategic Connectors (Envision-Activate preferences), the natural inclination is to focus on visionary ideas and engage people but not think enough about Design (what needs to happen when) and Build (how to best implement those priorities). When problems arise, Strategic Connectors, may ignore the possibility that priorities are not clear or that processes are weak, leading to fast starts and slow conclusions.

Cross-functional team members are typically wired to achieve similar goals in different ways. SP helps to manage this more productively, allowing people to see the bigger picture and move forward in a more integrated way. All fifteen Strategic Profiles relate to the same EDBA framework, making personal similarities and differences very easy to understand, communicate, and act upon.

SINGLE-DOMINANT STRATEGIC PROFILES

Profile	Preference	Velocity Implications
Visionary	Envision	Strong visionary. Works best when paired with Design, Build, and Activate people.
Designer	Design	Strong numerical orientation. Works best when direction is clear and when paired with Build and Activate people.
Builder	Build	Strong process orientation; works best when direction and priorities are clear (Envision, Design) and when paired with Activate people.
Activator	Activate	Strong interpersonal orientation; works best when direction, priorities, and processes are clear and when paired with Envision, Design, and Build people.

DOUBLE-DOMINANT STRATEGIC PROFILES

Profile	Preferences	Velocity Implications
Strategic Organizer	Envision and Build	Strong vision and process orientation; works best by not jumping into the how before the priorities are clear and by pairing with people who have strong Design and Activate skills.
Analytic Coach	Design and Activate	Strong quantitative and people orientation; works best when vision and processes are clear and by pairing with people who have strong Envision and Build skills.
Structured Worker	Design and Build	Strong "left brain" orientation, favoring objective numbers and processes; works best when the vision is clear and when paired with Envision and Activate people.
Strategic Connector	Envision and Activate	Strong strategic and interpersonal orientation; works best when priorities and processes are clear and when paired with Design and Build people.
Enterprise Thinker	Envision and Design	Strong conceptual orientation; works best when ideas can be put into practice with Build and Activate people.
Enterprise Worker	Build and Activate	Strong process and people skills; energized by actions more than concepts; works best when the vision and priorities are clear and when paired with Envision and Design people.

TRIPLE-DOMINANT STRATEGIC PROFILES

Profile	Preferences	Velocity Implications
Active Visionary	Envision, Build, and Activate	Strong vision, process, and people skills; works best when priorities are clear and when paired with Design people; needs to work on keeping EDBA sequenced.
Thinking Builder	Envision, Design, and Build	Strong vision, numerical, and process orientation; works best when fully engaged and when paired with Activate people; needs to work on keeping EDBA sequenced.
Active Designer	Design, Build, and Activate	Strong numerical, process, and people orientation; works best when the destination is clear and when paired with Envision people; needs to work on keeping EDBA sequenced.
Thinking Operator	Envision, Design, and Activate	Strong vision, numerical, and interpersonal orientation; works best when implementation is clear and when paired with Build people; needs to work on keeping EDBA sequenced.

QUADRUPLE-DOMINANT STRATEGIC PROFILE

Profile	Preferences	Velocity Implications
Holistic Worker	Envision, Design, Build, and Activate	Strong vision, numerical, process, and people preferences; needs to work very hard on keeping EDBA sequenced.

STRATEGIC PROFILE EXAMPLE: THE VISIONARY

Most people's profiles include combinations of EDBA prefer-ences, but the Visionary profile is singularly dominant in the Envision area. This could be the Captain Kirk on your team.

The Visionary

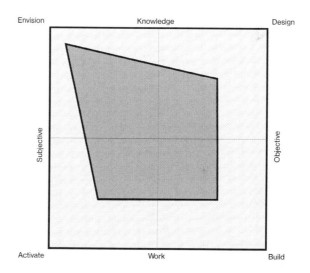

Visionaries solve problems intuitively. Envision characteristics include being creative, thinking strategically, creating a visionary destination, brainstorming, generating new ideas, seeing the big picture, and thinking inventively. Left alone, these out-of-the-box thinkers will often charge ahead despite having blind spots in areas such as analysis (Design), project management (Build), and collaboration (Activate). They are wired to think about *where*

to go and *why* in a given time frame—largely by instinct. To turn visions into actions, they need cross-functional team members and management routines such as SP-AP to help them connect the dots about *what* steps are needed *when* (Design), *how* these steps can be done best (Build), and *who* will be best qualified and motivated to implement these Build activities (Activate). If the EDBA steps are not connected, Envision people will not be as successful as they would otherwise be. This happens in many organizations that generate a lot of great ideas but have relatively few successful implementations.

SP helps manage these strengths and weaknesses by providing insights that help people collaboratively apply the EDBA framework, language, and process so that they can work together more productively to achieve better and faster outcomes. In the team version of SP, key insights are made visible that would otherwise be invisible. These include:

- individual and team strategic profiles;
- team and organizational strengths and weaknesses;
- key areas that require more emphasis;
- misconceptions about the team.

The ability to see and act on this information, in conjunction with SP-AP sessions, helps teams more systematically achieve better and faster outcomes.

EDBA IMPROVES CROSS-FUNCTIONAL OUTCOMES

The combination of a shared framework, language, and process; facilitated collaboration; and integrated project management helps teams systematically improve the velocity of key initiatives.

Even the best SP-AP plans in the world will struggle, however, if they are not implemented in an integrated way. Managing projects without basic discipline or with too much bureaucracy causes important initiatives to struggle during their implementations. To be more productive, key stakeholders need to integrate their efforts, and issues need to be escalated skillfully and solved collaboratively. Once SP-AP sessions produce cocreated solutions and integrated plans for moving forward, these plans then need to be project managed in a cross-functional way. This is where the EDBA project-management life cycle (PMLC) fits in.

EDBA HELPS PEOPLE TO MANAGE PROJECTS MORE PRODUCTIVELY

The velocity-advantage PMLC systematically turns good plans into successful outcomes. It helps cross-functional teams to productively orchestrate the efforts of the right people in the right way at the right time.

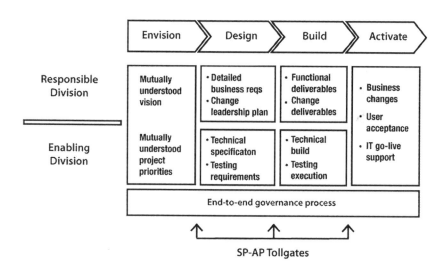

By integrating EDBA, SP-AP, and the velocity-advantage PMLC, teams can implement winning plans with greater velocity.

Cross-functional projects succeed when they have a shared vision, productive-planning capability, integrated governance, and the right skills applied at the right time. Effective collaboration, strong sponsorship, and good communication are also essential. Most initiatives also have change-management needs, and building these needs into the velocity-advantage PMLC is part of the design from the beginning.

In software development, many IT organizations use an approach that is referred to as "Agile." The velocity-advantage PMLC incorporates many of the same principles but at the organizational level. The planning process is shorter, there is less documentation, and there is continuous integration between the efforts of the stakeholders and the vision of the project. There is also a greater emphasis on collaboration, productively responding to change, and continuous improvement. With initiatives that require organizational change, Agile can be improved further when stakeholders use the EDBA language and process.

The EDBA-based PMLC helps organizations to successfully manage many of the key issues that make cross-functional projects fail. The problems addressed include unclear visions, poor communications, disjointed implementations, poorly resourced (too large and too small) project teams, inconsistent executive support, and the inability to make trade-off decisions.

Translated into a formula, the velocity advantage is captured by the following: EDBA (envision-design-build-activate) + SP-AP (strategic profiling—action planning) + PMLC (project-management life cycle) = VA (velocity advantage), or EDBA + SP-AP + PMLC = VA.

SP-AP IMPROVES CROSS-FUNCTIONAL LEADERSHIP SKILLS

One of the greatest benefits of SP-AP is that it improves leadership skills as a natural by-product of the EDBA collaborative process. A large cross section of people who have taken Strategic Profiling were interviewed and asked for their insights in three areas:

- What makes people effective and ineffective?
- What are the best and worst "boss behaviors?"
- What advice do you have for others?

The strategic profilers interviewed were from a variety of companies, including AT&T, Chubb, Intel, Infosys, Verizon, Lockheed Martin, the Coca-Cola Company, and Hilton Hotels. They included people with a variety of roles, including C-level executives, technology professionals, engineers, salespeople, and financial analysts. The interviewees also had a variety of different Strategic Profiles, with many EDBA preferences.

Strategic profilers have found that the most effective employees are focused, clear about their missions (and how they are going to get there), able to speak and adapt to different audiences, and skilled at building personal networks. They are results-oriented, have strong communication skills, and are excellent team players. Being ethical is also essential, as is having the ability to ask good questions. Effective people are generally seen as having a good sense of humor; they treat mistakes as opportunities, see the big picture, and are able to motivate and relate to people.

Ineffective leaders have large blind spots and struggle to relate well interpersonally. They are micromanagers, procrastinators, and excuse makers, and they are aggressive and more concerned with appearances and power than with accomplishment. They are also inconsistent, unrealistic, self-centered, paralyzed by analysis, and unable to act.

The best bosses are open, accountable, understanding, and communicative, and they have a positive ability to challenge others. They also encourage people to use their brains, give clear expectations for success, and are good at mentoring. They exude trust, respect, honesty, and ethical behavior. They are good teachers who help others learn the business while also learning more about themselves and others.

41

The worst bosses are micromanagers who execute poorly, treat people badly, and are negative and reactive. They are overly focused on how they look to their own bosses, often taking credit and shifting blame. Ineffective bosses do not let their people make decisions and are more interested in their own careers than in their organizations.

LEADERSHIP ADVICE FROM STRATEGIC PROFILERS

New employees: Be willing to work hard and learn; find your passion; have a good attitude; and be versatile, assertive, and a good listener. Be proactive and honest and ask questions. Have a good work ethic, be eager to collaborate, and do not be too aggressive. Be focused on the work and on the overall mission and goals of the organization.

Midlevel executives: Live in two worlds, coordinating and managing work with the front line *and* upper management. See the forest for the trees and be a good communicator. Focus, listen, and act with transparency and integrity. Do not micromanage or disconnect from your team and its goals.

Senior executives: Connect with people in a way that makes them feel valued as individuals and insiders. Do not get overly stressed, and accept certain levels of failure as being reasonable. Be caring and empathetic. Have passion, listen well, and exhibit high integrity. Do not stop interacting with the front line or be unapproachable. Do not hog the spotlight, micromanage, pretend you know everything, or be averse to risk. Do your homework and conscientiously and consistently invest time to inspect what you are expecting.

Highlights from "Activate Your Velocity Advantage"
SP-AP helps teams systematically build EDBA capabilities to cocreate winning solutions and integrated plans.
The first step is to identify an issue, choose the right team, design a facilitated session, and incorporate SP.
Building upon SP results, facilitated SP-AP sessions help teams rapidly cocreate winning solutions and integrated action plans and improve EDBA capabilities.
When the SP-AP step is complete, solutions can be productively implemented using the velocity advantage EDBA-based project-management life cycle (PMLC).
As velocity improves, people become better leaders – achieving better results, with stronger communication skills, and as better team players.

4

Step One – Envision Deep Dive

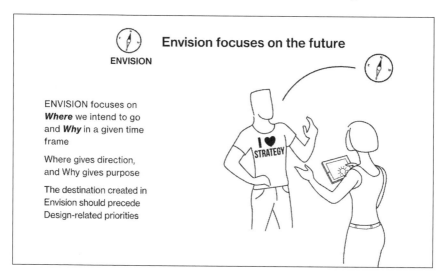

Envision focuses on the future

ENVISION

ENVISION focuses on **Where** we intend to go and **Why** in a given time frame

Where gives direction, and Why gives purpose

The destination created in Envision should precede Design-related priorities

Envision-oriented capabilities produce a compass and increase innovation in cross-functional initiatives. Part of the magic of Envision is the ability to create clear strategic destinations for where the group intends to go and why in a specific time frame. People will sometimes talk about two-pronged strategies. Beware. Avoiding choices usually results in organizational versions of Ditto the pig and the two-headed snake Thelma and Louise. Ditto was born with two mouths and two snouts and died from inhaling food into one while the other was eating. The heads of two-headed snakes fight each other over food and have trouble deciding which way to go; they are eventually eaten by predators. Cross-functional teams experience similar outcomes when strategic choices are not made or are unclear.

*   *   *

In Lewis Carroll's *Alice's Adventures in Wonderland*, the Cheshire Cat tells Alice that "If you don't know where you're going, any road'll take you there." Unfortunately, this is the default position with many cross-functional initiatives. Envision is the first step in the EDBA process and solves for this problem by helping teams cocreate shared destinations without wasted effort. It establishes *where* the team intends to go and *why* for a given *time frame* and is needed for small and large projects alike. In failing initiatives, single-minded and clearly stated destinations, shared purposes, and firm time frames are almost always missing.

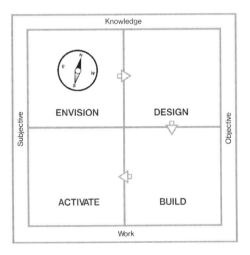

When the Envision step is not cocreated first by key stakeholders and used to guide cross-functional work, many dysfunctions occur. Without a clearly established Envision statement, people work hard without making much progress; difficulties arise from inconsistent and incompatible goals within and across functions; duplication of effort occurs; and critical projects eventually get delayed, scaled back, or stopped altogether.

IF YOU DON'T KNOW WHERE YOU'RE GOING...

Since people often solve problems and view success differently, teams are frequently not guided by a shared vision for success. In the tradition of scientific management, if something makes sense for someone's stand-alone piece and budget, that is often what matters most at the individual level. As a result, the activities related to *what, how,* and even *who* end up conflicting. This often wastes a lot of time and money. Jointly establishing *where* the cross-functional team intends to go and *why* for a given time frame is necessary before doing anything else. This step is often missed for a variety of reasons: stakeholders assume they agree on the destination when they really don't or they have different time frames in mind, use different words to describe the same things or the same words to talk about different things, and unconsciously (or not so unconsciously) protect their turf. The Envision step of the EDBA process helps people to get on the same page so that they can head in a single direction and implement and solve problems with greater quality and more productively. If the Envision step is not clear, I recommend considering a vacation. At least there is some value in a nice vacation.

The Envision step helps people cocreate a clear destination, purpose, and time frame. The *where* and *why* are both important. *Where* is the target, and *why* is the compass. If a company in the old days wanted to be the best buggy-whip maker in the world, it would have failed by successfully achieving its vision. Matched with the *why* of "to speed up transportation," the Envision statement could have helped the company more easily adapt in a changing environment.

The Envision statement helps cross-functional teams steer; it helps them productively achieve destinations and course-correct in an ever-changing world. When we work as consultants with large companies on project turnarounds, we always find that without this type of compass, the projects go off course, sometimes costing companies hundreds of millions of dollars.

Good Envision statements can fit on a T-shirt. They also push people out of their comfort zones, creating a fear of the status quo that is greater than the fear of the unknown. These visions for success are most effective when the dots are connected between where the organization has been, where it is today, and where it needs to go as well as why it needs to go there.

The value of a clear operational vision is timeless. Well before technology-enabled disrupters such as Jeff Bezos of Amazon and Mark Zuckerberg of Facebook came on the scene, entrepreneurs such as Sam Walton of Walmart and Ray Kroc of McDonald's also had very clear operating visions for their companies. They were masters at integrating their vision, plan, structure, and people to rapidly scale their organizations and disrupt their industries. Sam was a fanatic about eliminating waste. Ray was equally fanatical about quality, service, cleanliness, and value.

Winning Envision statements help stakeholders focus on the most important activities required to achieve them in the time frame required. They are not the same thing as "out-of-the-box" missions. In cross-functional initiatives, meaningful and cocreated Envision statements help organizations increase velocity and reduce "empty calories" by being integrated into the Design, Build, and Activate steps of the EDBA approach. Doing this correctly separates the ineffective dreamers from the successful implementers.

THE BEST WAY TO PREDICT THE FUTURE IS TO CREATE IT

Drucker told clients that the best way to predict the future was to create it. A clear cross-functional vision for where teams intend to go and why in a given time frame is the starting point for doing this, with an honest respect for history, a healthy discontent with the present, and a productive fear of the future. Articulating a clear destination and time frame helps teams develop winning game plans, capitalize on existing assets (including operational capabilities, customer relationships, and the executive team itself), write off the unneeded, and invest in the future. With a clearly articulated Envision statement, initiatives can adjust much more productively if they go off course or when the environment changes.

The Envision step helps teams produce better and faster outcomes through establishing a shared purpose before the rest of the work begins. This is extremely valuable, because each step of the EDBA process takes longer than the one before it. Design takes longer than Envision, Build takes longer than Design, and Activate takes longer than Build—and the entire EDBA cycle needs to be completed to produce a successful outcome. Every time the cycle is interrupted or disconnected, velocity decreases and scrap increases.

If executives change their minds while the organization is still working on the previous destination, much of the work that has been done on the previous vision will be wasted. This also happens when management shuffling produces changes in direction or when leaders don't lead or coordinate efforts from the top. Since knowledge is invisible, this waste does not get measured. It is costly nevertheless, and it eventually affects the company's results and market value. In today's organizations, the most unproductive situation of all is when there is no clear vision, priorities are not selected, and there is no good way to say no to competing ideas.

During the Envision step of the EDBA process, teams successfully cocreate shared destinations, purposes, and time frames for the work ahead. Good Envision statements then help organizations set priorities in the Design step. Great visions disrupt order to create it, thus helping organizations productively manage the proper balance between continuity and change.

ENVISION IS OUR COMPASS

With Envision as the strategic compass, it is much easier to innovate in a systematic way. Without doing this, choices are difficult to make, and companies are more likely to end up in the "nothing special" category. Systematic innovation incorporates the following questions:

- What's driving our business, now and in the future?
- Where should we invest to make the greatest impact?
- How can we build on our core strengths?
- What should we stop doing to make way for the new?

Planned abandonment is an important enabler for systematic innovation, since it helps companies to plant new trees for future profits and harvest mature trees to make way for them. These types of trade-offs increase sustainable growth rates and should be judged by the net value they produce (i.e., what is gained minus what is lost). They make superiority through differentiation possible through a healthy balance between cost reductions, investments in the future, and greater pricing power.

Innovation efforts fail when organizations perpetually brainstorm and don't pilot their best ideas. In many cases, the future is already here—it is simply not mainstream yet. Therefore, it's wise not to innovate for the future; innovate for the present. Start small and aim at leadership. As part of the innovation process, periodically put every established product, process, technology, market, distribution channel, and staff activity on trial for its life.

In large organizations, it is tempting to try to innovate in a vacuum to address or even try to create new customer needs.

Innovating *with* customers is a better way for companies to become more successful themselves by focusing on lowering cost structures, improving differentiation, and increasing velocity.

Systematic innovation requires organizational focus and deliberate trade-offs. To this end, companies can either concentrate their knowledge and diversify their products or concentrate their products and diversify their knowledge. This may require killing off or spinning off something that previously made the company great, which is why organized abandonment should be a core competency.

Innovation changes the wealth-producing potential of existing resources. Pacific Telesis did this when it incubated and launched AirTouch Communications (now part of Verizon). AirTouch was created within one of the most traditional companies on earth, as it was previously part of the Ma Bell telephone monopoly. CEO Sam Ginn saw the mobile opportunity, protected the new mobile group from the core organization, and then unleashed its potential through a public offering. This changed the wealth-producing potential of the company's existing resources and created substantial value for consumers, employees, and shareholders alike.

Copying the success of others can increase short-term revenue, but innovating your own path is a better option. Compare Apple and Dell from the time they were started: both were initially great success stories for their founders, but Apple consistently had a fraction of Dell's revenue and a far greater market value. Apple owned the secret sauce: its operating system and its incredible track record of exquisitely designed and integrated innovations.

The true test of innovation is not whether you personally like something but whether customers will pay for it. Successful innovations help companies sell more to existing customers, win over new customers, create successful new products and services, reinvent operational practices, and build productive alliances.

51

Companies can often solve their own problems by helping customers solve theirs. If you want to learn something, teach it. To get something, give it.

Good Envision statements reduce wasted effort

Strategic priorities can be selected and implemented much more productively when the destinations are clear and shared. Envision statements should *not* be highly detailed but should establish a clear difference between the current state and a more compelling future.

When the destination isn't clear in the Envision step, competing ideas become difficult to manage. Like an organizational version of the Whac-A-Mole game, a lot of energy is expended by people trying to sell new ideas and others working to whack them down. CIOs often struggle with this problem. New ideas frequently don't have a strategic purpose. As a result, technology portfolios often turn into a mishmash of applications that functional managers could not live without at one time or another but that are no longer important (or were never truly important at the start).

Simple Envision statements are best. The strategist Keniche Ohmae wrote that the inability to clearly articulate a strategy in a single sentence was a clear sign that there was something wrong with the strategy itself. In Hollywood, the same axiom applies to screenplays. Movie producers will say, "Give it to me in one sentence!" If you can't—if it takes you two or three sentences to get the main idea across—they know your script is not well plotted.

Every strategy has weaknesses; the worst ones try to be all things to all people. Good strategies require a clear destination, purpose, time frame, and tough choices. They help executives say no to otherwise good ideas that are off strategy.

There are many ways to think about strategy, and they can all be made more successful when linked to the EDBA process:

- A. G. Lafley and Roger Martin's *Playing to Win* process is powerful from a velocity-advantage perspective due to its collaborative nature and integration.
- Michael Porter's *Five Forces* strategy helps companies focus on rivalry, competitive entry, substitution, buyer power, supplier power, and value-chain analysis.
- The Stanford Research Institute's SWOT analysis helps companies focus on their **s**trengths, **w**eaknesses, **o**pportunities, and **t**hreats.
- The Boston Consulting Group's portfolio matrix is based on market share and growth to help firms analyze and identify "cash cows," "stars," "question marks," and "dogs."
- Various forms of stakeholder analyses can help companies examine strategic groups and their relationships to the firm.

Envision with customers, not for them

Market leadership does not cause competitive advantage; competitive advantage causes market leadership. Having strong customer relationships with cocreated visions for where you intend to go and why is critical. Concentrating on competitors versus customers will often result in price wars. Working *with* customers to lower their costs and make them more successful is a better approach, since it results in greater product-service differentiation, better personal relationships, "stickier" intellectual property, lower cost structures, and higher switching costs.

The goal is to achieve a clear direction that customers can see, a focused product and service offering that they prefer, an infrastructure that they depend upon, and relationships that they trust. Be memorable, meaningful, adaptable, and *protectable*. If everyone can do it, you won't be able to make a lot of money at it.

Guided by Envision, the Design step, which is the subject of the next chapter, answers the essential question, "*What* do you therefore need to do, and *when*, to implement your desired destination and purpose in a specified time frame?"

Key Characteristics of the "Envision" Step

Envision people often have a strong ability to visualize the future. A weakness is that they might not be interested enough in what is most important at the moment.

Envision characteristics include thinking strategically, creating a visionary destination, thinking inventively, generating new ideas, being creative, seeing the big picture, and brainstorming new ideas.

Highlights from "Step One — Envision Deep Dive"
By cocreating a clear destination, the Envision step answers "where we intend to go and why in a specified time frame."
Making the destination, purpose, and time frames clear helps organizations make better strategic choices.
Clear Envision statements increase velocity, whether you're working on a corporate strategy, implementing a cross-functional project, or planning a family vacation.
Innovation should focus on your customers – and be cocreated with customers when possible.
Determining where you intend to go and why should be memorable, meaningful, adaptable, and protectable.

5

Step Two – Design Deep Dive

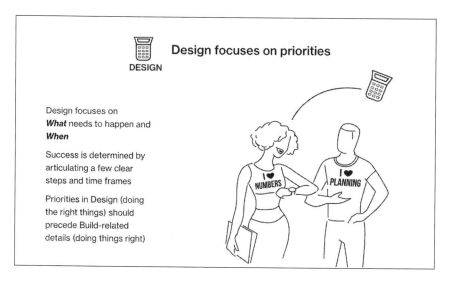

Design focuses on priorities

DESIGN

Design focuses on
What needs to happen and
When

Success is determined by
articulating a few clear
steps and time frames

Priorities in Design (doing
the right things) should
precede Build-related
details (doing things right)

I ♥ NUMBERS

I ♥ PLANNING

Analysis guided by a clear Envision statement is far more productive than trying to "boil the ocean." When the Envision statement is clear, priorities can be chosen with confidence in the Design step. Within EDBA, as a capability, Design (what needs to happen and when) includes activities such as planning, analysis, and measurement. Without a clearly articulated destination in Envision, analysis paralysis often consumes companies and projects alike. In Design, clear priorities increase cross-functional productivity, make analysis meaningful, and help companies adapt to changing environments via the EDBA process. New priorities start and old ones stop as visions and environments change. An important Design principle is that less is more—much more.

*   *   *

When Envision—where you intend to go and why in a given time frame—is clear, establishing *what* needs to happen and *when* it needs to happen becomes very straightforward in the Design step. If Envision and Design are not connected, priorities grow without a clear sense of direction, activity increases, and progress usually stalls. Where functions like marketing, research, and innovation are at home in the Envision world, Design is the sweet spot for functions like finance, accounting, planning, and engineering. Companies usually have good quantitative capabilities, since this is the foundation of MBA, CPA, and engineering programs. Analysis without a clear purpose, however, produces a lot of wasted effort, especially in areas like capital planning, financial analysis, and project management.

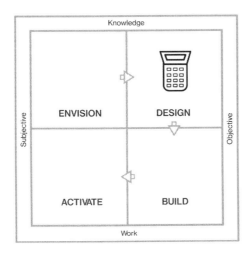

Some of the strengths of Design-oriented people and functions include the abilities to objectively prioritize, structure, measure, analyze, and plan. They are the most likely to "measure twice and cut once." As with Envision, Build, and Activate, this strength can also be a weakness in certain situations. Designers instinctively focus too much on numbers and not enough on the bigger picture behind those numbers. They can be brilliant with the parts yet miss the whole. Quoting Albert Einstein, "Not everything that can be counted counts."

Guided by a clear and shared destination in Envision, people with strong Design capabilities can help organizations increase their velocity by setting and monitoring the priorities that need to be implemented in the Build and Activate steps. Employees with strong Design capabilities are great at helping companies architect their product and service offerings, define and choose key initiatives, measure progress, and stay focused when it comes to the Build area.

ENOUGH IS AS GOOD AS A FEAST

As suggested earlier, organizations are not complex; they are complicated. Unlike machines, people are not wired to produce the same output from the same input. Different people react in a variety of ways to the same stimulus. Even the same person may react differently from one day to the next.

In the Design area, Peter Drucker created "management by objectives" (MBO), which helps people define and focus on the task, define results and quality, and establish accountability. Drucker intended MBO to be more humanistic than it eventually played out, but it is rooted in the objective-knowledge nature of Design.

As with all the other EDBA steps, Design is not an island; it is a bridge. It converts the output from Envision into a clear set of measurable priorities so that important implementation steps can be productively implemented in the Build and Activate steps.

Focus increases the power of Design. During a turnaround situation at Coca-Cola Beverages in Canada, after its stock price had fallen by more than half and the company was losing a million dollars a week, we focused on a few key activities and measures.

All our marketing, financial, operational, and sales measures were limited to ten one-page reports. If a measure was not on one of those reports, then we did not use it in management meetings. Local operators sometimes resisted this strategy because it limited their flexibility when the key indicators weren't good. Nonetheless, we stayed the course because this helped us focus and integrate the company's efforts. We celebrated together when the measures were good. When the measures were not good, we jointly worked on problem solving.

When I was CFO at Coca-Cola Beverages, we also found that less was more with investment analysts. The clearer our measures became, the more focused the company became and the easier it was for investors to understand our value proposition. We focused on a few areas—economic value added, gross-profit growth, SG&A (selling, general, and administrative expense) percentage, return on assets, and free cash flow—linked to five clearly articulated strategic initiatives. This approach worked very well. The market value of the company increased sevenfold in five years.

With Design, as with other EDBA steps, it is important to keep the bigger picture in mind. In today's data-rich world, it is easy for managers to become so focused on the parts that they lose sight of the whole. By focusing on the pennies, employees can lose sight of the dollars. To paraphrase Oscar Wilde, we end up knowing the price of everything without knowing the value of anything.

Skipping dollars to save pennies—by not seeing the bigger picture—happens when Design-oriented people do not factor in the value of time. As a consultant, I once watched a company take a year and a half to analyze and negotiate a $1 million-per-week multiyear savings opportunity. Had time been factored in, it would have been clear that the $3 million the company saved through extensive price negotiations came at a $75 million opportunity cost. Sadly, the procurement officer viewed this result as a success on his department's scorecard.

This also occurs when companies strive for "lower blended rates" with professional services firms. When companies embrace this approach, they inevitably exchange a larger number of low-priced people for fewer high-priced people. Fewer high-priced people almost always get better results, and in shorter time frames. First, they have more experience and less of a learning curve. Second, significantly lower coordination costs are involved, especially if some resources are onshore and others offshore. As will be described in the next chapter, the coordination cost for ten people is forty-five times higher than the coordination cost for two people. Less is more.

Focusing on the bigger picture helps executive teams resist the temptation to cut costs in isolation, especially when the real problem is an outdated business model. This mistake has reoccurred throughout business history. In retailing, Woolworth did not break away from Main Street when Sears entered the malls. Kmart took over from Sears with its city orientation but was then unable to beat Walmart when Sam Walton moved in from the rural areas. Then came Amazon and the revolution of online retailing more generally. With watches, the Swiss took over market-share leadership from the United Kingdom with the first pocket watch. Then the United States began selling more watches by producing them with machines. The Swiss took over again with more stylish machine-produced watches, and Japan took over with quartz watches. Now, smartphones and wearable computer devices are replacing traditional watches altogether. With technology, IBM lost the PC profit pool to Microsoft because IBM considered itself a hardware company when Bill Gates' company emerged and saw the PC as a software opportunity. Microsoft subsequently lost the web opportunity to Google. Microsoft viewed the web through its desktop, whereas Google saw the potential value of connecting Internet searches, eyeballs, and advertising. Facebook then capitalized on the social connections associated with those eyeballs, and so on.

Focusing on the trees instead of the forest is a common blind spot of Design-oriented people and functions. While trying to make existing business models more efficient, disruptive competitors implement new value propositions altogether. Sticking with established practices is part of human nature because new approaches usually don't fit in with our preestablished mental models. This is one reason why planned abandonment is important and why it helps to connect the objective nature of Design with the more subjective and forward-thinking nature of Envision.

In organizations, the not-to-do list is more important than the to-do list. Without focus, it is very easy to get consumed by the details and lose sight of what's most important—like the recreational chess player versus the grand master described in the second chapter. Details are very important, but as Mary Poppins told young Michael Banks, "Enough is as good as a feast."

THE FOUNDATION OF DESIGN: LESS IS MORE

Making choices during the Design step increases velocity during the Build and Activate steps. Shared Envision statements make this possible. It's common sense but sometimes lost in the heat of the battle: if the destination and time frame are clear in Envision, then it's much easier to set the right priorities in Design and execute them more successfully in Build and Activate.

A few key priorities help organizations and their cross-functional teams produce faster and higher-quality outcomes. This type of focus requires constant vigilance, because it is human nature to try to do too many things at one time. Velocity increases when organizations have the discipline to focus on a few key priorities and a core set of metrics.

"Less is more" also applies to planning. General Dwight D. Eisenhower said that plans were nothing, but planning was everything. Large companies can learn from small ones in this area. When plans fail in small companies, the marketplace forces those plans—and sometimes the companies themselves—to die. In large companies, bad plans get life support from fixed internal budgets, which makes it harder to successfully adapt to ever-changing environments.

In the EDBA process, the Envision step helps companies and cross-functional teams cocreate a clear destination so that a focused set of priorities can be established in the Design step. Doing this helps companies and teams focus on the right things at the right time and direct scarce human, capital, and technological resources to the most fruitful areas.

GOOD ORGANIZATIONAL LOGIC INCREASES VELOCITY

Poor organizational logic causes many Design problems in large companies. It is very difficult for people to be productive when EDBA is out of whack at the company level. Strong Design expertise can help improve organizational logic—and companies overall—in four key areas:

- product-service menus
- hierarchy and decisions
- incentive designs
- centralization-decentralization

PRODUCT-SERVICE MENUS ARE FOUNDATIONAL

Whether they know it or not, every company has a product-service menu. This plays out very naturally in restaurants and is an easy example to conceptualize. In a restaurant, the product-service menu helps focus business activities for customers, employees, and suppliers alike. If a restaurant did not have a menu, then servers, kitchen personnel, and suppliers would not be able to productively do their jobs. The restaurant's operations would be chaotic, and patrons would have unmet expectations.

Executives do not typically think about their companies this way, so product-service menus are usually not clear (if they exist at all). This misallocates scarce resources. A well-designed product-service menu helps organizations operate more successfully. If companies cannot define themselves, then they will get negatively defined by more focused competitors and increasingly confused customers.

The value of clear product-service menus is most obvious with start-ups. To win and scale their businesses, start-ups need to design their value propositions very clearly and be explicit about what their organizations do and do not do. If new companies aren't focused, then it is hard to be good at—or known for—anything specific.

Trying to be all things to all people may feel safer, but just the opposite is actually true. Well-designed product-service menus help companies focus, become better integrated, and achieve higher rates of continuous improvement. Being great at the basics is a winning practice, and the basics can get stronger faster with clear designs. Through strong design choices, good things happen by doing fewer things better and in a more integrated way.

HIERARCHY AND DECISIONS ARE CROSS-FUNCTIONAL PLUMBING

Organizational charts tell a story. While it is possible for large companies to work worse than their organizational designs, they can never work better. In the invisible and fluid world of today's organizations, structure matters more than ever. In addition to basic organizational hierarchy, ad hoc capabilities are needed to systematically bring the right people together at the right times to achieve the best cross-functional outcomes. This ad hoc capability is integrated into SP-AP and is one reason why it is so effective.

Clear decision rights are also an important by-product of good organizational logic, in routine as well as ad hoc situations. Having good decision architectures in place significantly improves an organization's velocity and ability to adapt; it helps to set priorities, make trade-off decisions, help employees reach their goals, and make planned-abandonment choices.

In many companies, it is common to hear complaints about executives being unable to make timely decisions. In defense of the executives, they frequently don't get the request for a decision in an actionable form. Employees often assume that their bosses know more than they actually do about required decisions, and bosses assume that they will be asked for their help in clear terms when needed. Decision making and problem solving often struggle because both sides don't know what they don't know.

Well-designed organizational logic helps companies avoid the dark side of striving for consensus. Consensus can be difficult with two people. With ten, it is impossible. Consensus has become the anaconda of organizations. The anaconda does not bite. It kills its prey through suffocation. Striving for consensus produces committees, most of which struggle to make decisions—especially when choices benefit one party at the expense of another. Without making these choices, organizations chase "shiny objects": they work on too many projects (all of which require resources) without getting enough done.

A key purpose of organizational hierarchies is to make choices when consensus fails. Bottom-up input provides decision makers with better knowledge, but input is not a decision right. By proactively separating "trade-off makers" from "input givers," companies can move faster. No choice is perfect, but it is much better to implement something imperfectly than to do nothing flawlessly.

The lack of clear decision-making architectures is usually only one part of the problem. Communication style is another. People on the front line often do not think or talk in terms of decisions. They think and talk in terms of problems. This situation is made more difficult because bosses often do not have the subject-matter expertise of the person who's doing the work. As a result, bosses are usually not in the best position to solve problems. They *are*, however, in an excellent position to make decisions—with greater organizational power and a broader view. Even though decision making is different from problem solving, good decisions end up solving problems.

Explicit decision rights and well-established escalation rules help organizations increase velocity. Without having these in place, too many people feel entitled to delay a decision; who is entitled to make one is not clear enough. In large organizations, decision makers need to be given a short problem statement that includes two or three alternative decisions, with expected implications. Articulating an explicit recommendation is also essential.

Delegation rules are also important. If a decision is well within the boundaries of what the boss controls, and she knows the most about the subject, then it is usually best not to delegate it. Delegation is best when decisions are routine or when the employee has more expertise in the subject area. Delegation should not turn into abdication. Delegated decisions need to be a joint effort between the boss and the expert. Otherwise, good decisions will not be made, nor will they stick.

In the words of Napoleon Bonaparte, nothing is as difficult or as precious as making decisions. Decisions are hard because they limit our options, but the clarity of the resulting choices helps to channel the right resources in the right areas at the right times. Decisions move companies toward their future visions and are essential to the Design EDBA bridge from Envision to Build. Doing this with speed and direction requires the combination of a clearly constructed hierarchy, clear decision rights, and a strong ability to escalate.

INCENTIVE DESIGNS ARE AN UNDERUTILIZED ASSET

Most people are not in a position to directly influence their company's incentive design, but it is a very important choice at the corporate level or when starting a new company. "Less is more" applies here as well; incentives are best when linked to a small but holistic set of goals. When too many activities are incentivized, the incentive system loses its power. Incentive structures require choices, rewarding certain priorities at the expense of others.

Companies commonly incentivize functional performance *and* corporate performance. This is not a major problem with industrial work, because the parts are stable and distinct. It's more of a problem with knowledge organizations, which have a high degree of interdependence between individuals and groups. For example, the CFO may espouse that he or she wants to build a world-class finance organization. If finance is not the company's bottleneck, however, then strategically investing there will misallocate resources for the company overall. In an extreme case, the company could go out of business despite having the world's best financial capabilities.

Interdependence is found across business units and functions. Marketing, sales, and the supply chain all affect one another. The incentive structure should be designed in a way to help ensure that when choices are made, the company benefits overall.

Incentives are not only about money. There are three basic types:

- zero-sum incentives (e.g., position in a hierarchy)
- limited incentives (e.g., compensation)
- unlimited incentives (e.g., recognition)

Incentive structures are often designed based on what worked in the industrial age. They are linked to hierarchy, and within hierarchical levels, there is relatively little difference between what a high performer and a moderate performer earn. Personal contribution, though, varies significantly between people in today's organizations. A computer-programming genius can be thousands of times more productive than an average programmer. Yet they both have similar job titles and salary ranges. Since what is going on in their heads is invisible, one may seem pretty much the same as the other to their human-resources manager. The one with the best attitude will often have an edge, regardless of personal competence.

To improve velocity, incentive structures should be decoupled from organizational hierarchy in some cases. Having dual career ladders in technical functions is one illustration of this. Examples may also be found in certain industries: when movie stars earn more than directors, advertising-agency general managers earn less than creative directors, professional athletes earn more than coaches, and college coaches earn more than university presidents.

If someone contributes ten times more than someone else in the same department—and this is possible in certain roles—then incentive designs should do a better job of accommodating this difference. This is the norm in direct sales and can be tailored when incentivizing jobs that benefit from extraordinary levels of expertise. Winning organizations will attract and keep better people by turning employees into partners, and incentive structures should be used to help companies do this. The alternative is that the best people will not stay or will not join in the first place.

CENTRALIZATION-DECENTRALIZATION LINES NEED TO BE CLEAR

Another organizational logic driver is where centralization and decentralization lines are drawn. Different designs produce different advantages and disadvantages, and each choice has organizational winners and losers. There are also internal winners and losers each time the centralization-decentralization lines change. Decentralized organizations are well suited to autonomous and spontaneous local operations. Centralized companies are better at getting enterprise-wide synergies and acting as a unified force across geographies and business lines. With centralized operations, functions usually have the last word; in decentralized organizations, general managers do. Regardless of where the lines are drawn, making them logically consistent increases velocity.

Centralization-decentralization lines should also be considered with respect to how capital is controlled. There are certain advantages to controlling capital centrally in decentralized organizations to ensure that operators don't go on spending sprees or make bad choices. Yet this can bog companies down.

The time wasted on traditional capital-management processes can be significant. Large companies can take a full year between when someone identifies a capital need to when the ultimate decision is made. Then it can take an additional year or more to receive the equipment or build what's needed. As a result, nimbler competitors can implement something before slower companies have obtained an authorization to move forward; these delays are often the result of organizational-logic issues between finance and operations.

NUMBERS NEED CONTEXT

Design capabilities are based on objectivity and quantification, but there are sometimes differences between the numbers and what is behind those numbers. Businesses are living ecosystems, while numbers are frozen snapshots. Figures are important, but they're like the mounted deer mentioned earlier, whereas the business is like a living one.

Early in my career, I was the chief marketing officer for the Coca-Cola Bottling Company of New England when New Coke was introduced. The facts were clear that most people preferred the taste of New Coke to the original formula. Research conclusively showed that 55 percent versus 45 percent favored it, which was very significant, given the power of the brand and size of the category. When the formula was changed, the truth was that, despite the facts, many consumers did not want to buy it. The original formula was reintroduced as Coca-Cola Classic.

When people focus only on the numbers, it can turn into spreadsheet management, where the spreadsheet's "what-if" calculations seem to become more real than the business itself. Rather than executives managing the numbers, the numbers begin to manage the executives. Great companies don't make money; they make products and services that customers buy. First, they win in the marketplace, and then they earn more money as a result.

The contextual side of Design is also important with data analytics in today's world of "big data." In practice, successful analytics outcomes are socio-systematic. To be a transformative force, some important (but often missing) human requirements are necessary:

- Open discussions are required on the limits of analytics, when to trust intuition, and how to blend the art and science of business decision making.
- Top-down business modeling with executives is needed to combine knowledge and data in the best way possible. Experienced IT executives are an integral part of the equation but are not the only constituency.
- Two-way communication is necessary but often missing. Business leaders need to know the basic concepts of analytics, and the analytics team needs to be able to speak and understand the language of business.

Throughout this chapter, the Design step in the EDBA process has been described as the bridge between Envision and Build. The Build step—focused on implementing projects, systems, processes, and infrastructure—is also essential for the velocity advantage and is the subject of the next chapter.

Key Characteristics of the "Design" Step

Design-oriented people are great with numbers, priorities, plans, and measures. A weakness is that they can sometimes not see the forest for the trees.

Design characteristics include analyzing situations; establishing clear rules, detailed objectives, and clear measures; making detailed plans; being objective; and making decisions by the numbers.

Highlights from "Step Two – Design Deep Dive"

The Design step helps turn the Envision statement into a clear and objective set of priorities.

Companies win by making smart choices, doing a few things well, and doing them in the right sequence.

Having clear product-service menus helps organizations win through better focus, integration, and constancy of purpose.

Organizational logic increases velocity through unified structures, good decision architectures, productive incentives, and clear centralization-decentralization lines.

Numbers need context. They should not be mistaken for the destination. Be careful not to mistake measures for goals.

6

Step Three – Build Deep Dive

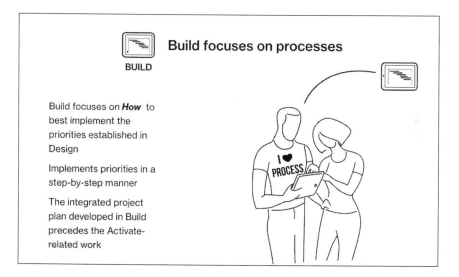

Build focuses on processes

BUILD

Build focuses on **How** to best implement the priorities established in Design

Implements priorities in a step-by-step manner

The integrated project plan developed in Build precedes the Activate-related work

The Build-related capabilites in the EDBA process help large organizations to productively implement the priorities established in Design. Build capabilities are a common blind spot in today's companies, and complicated operations, weak project management, and ineffective IT systems are common symptoms. In the Oliver Wendell Holmes poem "The One-Hoss Shay," Holmes wrote about a buggy that needed no repairs for more than a hundred years. The buggy then collapsed into a heap in a single instant. The Build capabilities are critical to sustainability because companies can go from apparent success to failure when systems, processes, and infrastructure don't keep up with competitors.

*   *   *

Through Strategic Profiling, we track and analyze people's preferences for a variety of Envision, Design, Build, and Activate characteristics. As it turns out, weakness in the Build area is usually the biggest blind spot, often by quite a bit.

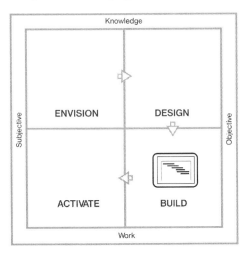

While clients always agree that implementation skills are important, Build-oriented capabilities often get glossed over, especially by senior executives. Two symptoms are that project management and systems-integration capabilities are almost always weak. When companies experience implementation problems, executives—because of Build blind spots—often react by trying to change their strategies (Envision), asking for more analyses (Design), or hiring different people (Activate). This then generates a lot of activity with very little progress, since it doesn't address the core issue. Build, like Envision, Design, and Activate, is both a step within and a capability of the velocity-advantage EDBA process. Evidence of strong Build capabilities can be seen when companies have excellent processes, successful projects, sufficient standardization, well-integrated systems, and good infrastructure.

Build-oriented functional areas include logistics, manufacturing, information systems, and project management. As individuals, Builders are good at productively implementing priorities. They are great organizers (often with clean desks) with a natural ability to implement and integrate critical initiatives, standard processes, and step-by-step procedures. This strength can also be a weakness, as strong Build-oriented people are inclined to resist changes in direction due to their appreciation for the tried and true. Companies with strong Build capabilities are operationally excellent, with consistent customer interfaces and lower infrastructure costs compared to their less systematic competitors.

To achieve a velocity advantage, the Build step should be directly linked to the Envision, Design, and Activate steps. Like the cart in "The One-Hoss Shay," if Build is not connected to the bigger EDBA picture, then companies will not be able to adapt. This has been the case throughout business history. The late Apple cofounder Steve Jobs once walked through a state-of-the-art IBM dot-matrix-printer facility (the predecessor of the laser printer) when he was a young man. After the tour, he commented that the factory was very impressive but was making the wrong stuff. It is useless to do something efficiently that should not be done at all. It's important to determine the right things in Envision and Design and then do them right in Build and Activate. Companies can do more business with lower structural costs, and implement priorities better and faster, by having strong Build capabilities.

ORGANIZATION TURNS PRIORITIES INTO OUTCOMES

Napoleon Hill, a self-help author, interviewed people in the early 1900s who had earned large personal fortunes. He discovered that knowledge became power when it was organized and put into action.

Through strong Build competencies, companies use cross-functional project management to turn business priorities into strong business capabilities. Build is the bridge from Design to Activate. Just like with Envision and Design, Build requires clear choices. This sometimes gets teams stuck. It is natural for people to want to do everything well, but different options usually have something wrong with them. The key is to embrace imperfection and then continually iterate.

Through Build, good internal integration produces strong external capabilities. Moving forward successfully in a step-by-step manner is embedded in the Build capability. Making choices on whether the disadvantages of standardization (i.e., lack of flexibility) are greater than the advantages (i.e., more synergy, consistency, and scalability) comes with the territory.

When their Build capabilities are weak, organizations struggle with quality, cost, and speed issues. This happens a lot with project management in general and systems in particular and seems to be getting worse at many companies. By trying to get systems implemented faster, nontechnologists have increasingly taken things into their own hands, often encouraged by the sales arms of external consultants and vendors. This causes longer-term security, standardization, scalability, and operational issues. On the other hand, when project management and IT people and functions resist change too much, or can't communicate the benefits of (and convince leaders to enforce) standard-technology architectures, they hold companies back through competency traps. The velocity-advantage process helps organizations find and implement a better balance between vision and structure.

The focus of Build is on process, integration, and systems. Culturally, problems in the Build area are usually easy to spot because bad behaviors produce bad systems, and good behaviors, like productive collaboration and effective project-selection capabilities, go hand in hand with good ones.

The importance of the Build area became very clear to me when Coca-Cola Enterprises was created in the mid-1980s. The company was formed as a single publicly traded entity after combining several large US bottling companies. During this time, I received an excellent education on why it is crucial to connect the dots between the EDBA steps. When these previously independent entities came together, the inconsistencies between operational areas became painfully clear.

At the new company, functional leaders were asked to design their organizations as they saw fit. Incompatible structures and systems soon emerged, making it very difficult to coordinate activities at the local level. As the original head of the distribution area, I advocated a national supply chain with fewer warehouses, less inventory, and fewer transportation miles. But this meant that manufacturing costs would need to increase to reduce overall supply-chain costs. Meanwhile, the head of manufacturing was asked to focus intensely on the company's production costs and not to worry about overall supply-chain costs or asset intensity. What our boss believed was creative tension was, from a Build perspective, pure and simple structural incongruence.

During my next job, I was able to manage the entire supply chain for Coca-Cola Beverages. The CEO, William P. Casey, ensured that the executive team was integrated, and he forced trade-off decisions when we were not. Major changes happened quickly, in every function and across the company. For his success, Casey was named *Beverage Industry Magazine*'s Executive of the Year.

FOCUS IMPROVES "BUILD" CAPABILITIES

Focus is important within and across all four EDBA steps, but this is especially true in the Build area. In the same way that having good brakes makes it safer to drive cars faster, with clearer project management, governance, systems, and processes, organizations can move faster and with less risk.

Adopting and applying the following five techniques, which will be covered in greater detail next, are a great way to help teams and organizations improve and benefit from strong Build capabilities:

- the Pareto principle
- Metcalfe's law
- workflow queue reduction
- constraint management
- integrated projects

THE PARETO PRINCIPLE

The Pareto principle, also known as the 80/20 rule, was developed by the Italian economist Vilfredo Pareto in the mid-nineteenth century. This principle is very useful in the Build area because a small percentage of activities often produces a large percentage of the overall value in critical business areas. The 80/20 rule has broad application. A large percentage of a company's revenue often comes from a small percentage of products, services, and customers. A large percentage of an organization's transaction costs usually comes from a small percentage of the firm's revenue. Companies can improve significantly by applying the 80/20 rule to their activities. Conversely, if a company tries to be everything to everyone, then the 80/20 rule will work against the organization overall.

Applying the 80/20 rule to itself is a particularly powerful exercise. The continual application of the 80/20 rule to the top 20 percent leads to the possibility that the top 1 percent can potentially generate three times more value than the bottom 80 percent; the top 20 percent more than one hundred times the value of the bottom 51 percent.

Economic results are usually proportional to revenue, while costs are proportional to the number of transactions. We applied this in practice at Coca-Cola Beverages and found that 50 percent of our SKUs ("stock keeping units," i.e., product-package combinations) represented only 3 percent of our volume. By discontinuing these products, we produced more volume with only half the manufacturing facilities—and with 35 percent less inventory. From a marketing perspective, doing this also freed up capacity to launch more new products and increase excitement in the marketplace.

Continually applying the 80/20 rule can help organizations determine how to best phase out underperforming products and services and invest in more fruitful areas in order to attain new levels of performance. Introducing new products and services, funded by discontinued nonperforming ones, is equivalent to a business version of "the circle of life."

METCALFE'S LAW

Where the 80/20 rule helps to focus efforts on the most important value drivers, Metcalfe's law, or the N formula, helps people actively manage organizational complexity. The formula is $(N^2 - N) \div 2$.

The implications are often eye-opening. If you and I were working on a project, we would have one communication flow between us. Using the N formula, this can be easily calculated as $2 \div 2 = 1$. As the number of people involved grows larger, the degree of difficulty skyrockets.

If we increase the size of a team from two to three people—a 50 percent increase—the difficulty factor doesn't go up by the same 50 percent. It goes up by 200 percent. If a team expands from two people to ten, this does not increase difficulty by five times but by forty-five times.

The N formula can help organizations proactively manage the degrees of difficulty associated with having too many cooks in the kitchen. The N formula makes the productivity power of involving the right people at the right time more understandable and manageable, including the value of having fewer decision makers and smaller teams.

Having smaller teams significantly increases the velocity of important cross-functional initiatives. For example, in a $1 billion business-technology project that our team was brought in to help on, the company's executives instinctively believed that since this project cost a lot of money, maximum involvement was needed. After struggling for two years, it ended up being much better to look at the initiative as a $500,000-per-day project, with each two-week delay—due to having too many of the wrong people involved—resulting in an additional $5 million cost. After grinding continually, the project's governance structure went from 120 people to the most appropriate three executives. The project improved immediately. Using the N formula makes it much easier to better focus initiatives up front. Velocity improves when there are fewer—but the right—cooks in the kitchen.

One person we interviewed for the book put it this way: "Today I worked with ten people from our consulting firm, and we accomplished very little. When I worked for a small firm, I could personally accomplish all that the larger team was supposed to do. Before, when I left for the day, I knew the difference I had made. Now, the days never end, and getting things done takes forever."

QUEUE REDUCTION

Queues are like checkout lines in supermarkets. In organizations, they absorb time and money in subtle but significant ways. For example, if a work deliverable takes two hours for someone to complete, but it is at the bottom of his or her two-week-long inbox or e-mail queue, then it will take two weeks and two hours to complete what could have taken only two hours. Put four of these transactions together, and it takes two months to do what could have been done in one day. With factory work, these disconnects can be easily seen and corrected, but with large cross-functional teams, this is more difficult to manage.

Queue management is the basis for the just-in-time (JIT) inventory systems used in the manufacturing world. JIT removes safety stock so that underlying inefficiencies can be better seen and fixed, which then helps manufacturers remove safety stock on a permanent basis.

Queues in organizations are like safety stock in factories. They crop up for a variety of reasons. Sometimes people have no awareness that something is important, while at other times, the parties involved have no shared priorities. Making cross-functional interdependencies more visible through SP-AP and process mapping are two ways to help manage queue problems. It also helps when cross-functional teams replace geographically based meetings—where everyone has to be in the same location at the same time—with the productive use of asynchronous communications. Faster escalation and simpler governance structures are other ways to better manage queues.

One way to reduce queues is to identify situations where individuals become more productive by making the whole less productive. Prioritizing work at the individual level often reduces an organization's or project's overall productivity. Something relatively unimportant to an individual can be very important to the company overall because of the interdependence of cross-functional work.

When people are part-time subject-matter experts, for example, the assignment is usually not the most important part of their jobs, and they may give it a low personal priority for that reason. But even though they may be improving their personal productivity by not being responsive to requests, their actions suboptimize the bigger picture. With large initiatives, someone who earns $100,000 per year can seriously, and often unknowingly, delay projects that cost more than $100,000 per day.

Responding to people's requests right away helps eliminate queues. This usually improves the individual's productivity as well. If you respond to people immediately, then those who depend on you won't absorb your time in other ways, by filling up your inbox, repeatedly leaving you messages, copying you and those who influence you on too many e-mails, scheduling recurring meetings just to get face time, and getting you on a committee to ensure periodic involvement. Improving personal-response times can pay great dividends. I began practicing this when I had personal-productivity issues, and my e-mails and meetings eventually went down by more than 50 percent.

Even though recurring meetings are a common practice in many of today's large organizations, they can significantly increase queues and strangle the life out of people's calendars. As an alternative, when managing queues, short e-mails or texts should be used for simple communications, with live conversations reserved for when the subject is more complicated. A five-minute conversation will often eliminate the need for dozens of e-mail or text interactions or for scheduled meetings. Face-to-face meetings are better when an important change is required, but a phone conversation or a conference call can also be extremely productive when people are in different locations. People inevitably find that velocity breeds even greater velocity, with queues continually reduced in the process.

MANAGING CONSTRAINTS UNLOCKS POTENTIAL

In his book *The Theory of Constraints*, the late business author Eliyahu Goldratt made a compelling case that when everyone works on their piece of the system 100 percent of the time, the overall system becomes inefficient. One area produces too much, while another area is short of resources. By focusing on the bottlenecks, total output improves.

As people work on nonbottlenecks, resources get misallocated. To make matters worse, they commonly enlist others to help them with these nonbottlenecks. Managing constraints is important to cross-functional initiatives because, in changing environments, they signal the need for resources—for the good of the entire system. The existence of bottlenecks signals that a priority is being constrained. By identifying and staffing bottlenecks—funded by nonbottleneck resources—companies become more productive overall.

To effectively manage these situations, it is important to focus on the big picture so that resources can be prioritized on an ad hoc basis to solve bottlenecks as they arise. This requires productive collaboration (such as with SP-AP and collaborative process mapping) in addition to very clear governance structures. After teams solve one bottleneck, another one will emerge; then the new bottleneck will need to be addressed. Given the interdependent nature of cross-functional work, bottlenecks need to be continually solved to productively allocate and reallocate scarce resources. By continually identifying and managing constraints, teams can consistently work on those things that matter most.

SUCCESSFUL CROSS-FUNCTIONAL PROJECTS INCREASE VELOCITY

The traditional project-management approach was designed for stable environments and developed using scientific-management principles. The approach incorporates extensive analysis and preplanning, breaks stable bodies of work into its component parts, and then helps to independently manage those parts. When external consultants are in charge, the process often goes a step further and leverages, in machinelike fashion, junior consultants, who follow templates that were designed for other organizations. To make matters worse, consulting economics improve as a result of up-front analyses, change orders, and overruns. In defense of the consulting industry, significant change usually does not happen without external assistance and expertise, because employees often have agendas, are limited by their place in the hierarchy (both high and low), and are consumed by their day jobs.

Cross-functional projects struggle when they are managed this way using approaches that date back to Henry Gantt and the early 1900s. Gantt, an associate of Frederick Taylor, created procedures such as work-breakdown structures to logically separate activities into visible, independent, and predictable activities. Some of this approach is still very relevant in cross-functional projects, including the need to manage scope, quality, cost, and time. Objectives also need to be SMART: specific, measurable, achievable, realistic, and time-bound. While these ideas are sound, cross-functional projects regularly fail to deliver on their initial expectations using this approach, which is why a socio-systematic approach like the velocity advantage is needed.

Traditional project-management techniques work very well when projects do not have a lot of change and human complication. When a lot of organizational dynamics are involved, however, the traditional approach often struggles to deliver. Despite the best intentions, scientifically managed cross-functional projects usually take too long and cost too much. When projects struggle, human complications and EDBA process problems always contribute. Envision statements are not clear, governance structures are missing or overengineered, and employees and consultants are working on the *how* before they have decided *where* they intend to go and *why* and *what* the priorities are. The projects struggle with unresolved disconnects between stakeholders who find it difficult to collaborate because they don't share a common language, vision, or process.

Successful cross-functional projects don't operate the same way as highly structured initiatives and software development. The traditional approach often fails to compensate for weak governance, unclear priorities, decisions that aren't made properly, visions that are at odds, and personality conflicts. With these types of projects, failure rates are high, collaboration is unproductive, and project management isn't tailored to the situation. There is too much analysis and not enough decision making. Too much "big bang" planning and not enough piloting. Too much meeting and not enough collaboration. Too much inclusion and not enough accountability.

THE VELOCITY ADVANTAGE HELPS BUSINESSES TRANSFORM

There are several things to be learned from failed cross-functional transformation initiatives. These projects fail when they are overmanaged and underled and have incompatible visions for success, visions that aren't executable, weak decision making, and poorly integrated project-management processes.

Trying to force fit templates that were designed for other companies is another common issue. While using this strategy helps teams to get started quickly and feels very complete at the beginning, it often runs into trouble later when the template is incompatible with the organization that's trying to adopt it. In effect, project teams try to build new houses that are incompatible with the current home's underlying structure. It's not wise to try to turn a four-bedroom colonial into a five-bedroom ranch.

Several things are needed for cross-functional transformational initiatives to be successful. First, the stakeholders need to cocreate the transformation strategy (i.e., get in the same room) so that it can be implemented productively. Doing this reduces risk, increases speed, and helps the initiatives better adapt to changing environments. Second, productive governance capabilities with a few key people are needed at both the company and work-stream levels. Third, an integrated PMLC is necessary to unify and sequence the work. Fourth, the project structure needs to match the work to be done—understanding that employees have a business to run and that rapid access to subject-matter expertise and organizational power are nonnegotiable conditions for success.

COCREATING INITIATIVES UP FRONT IMPROVES END RESULTS

Executive sponsors should strongly resist the urge to jump into implementations before they believe that the project stakeholders have agreed to a single implementation approach that can succeed and evolve as conditions change. This is an important reason for the use of executive-level SP-AP sessions before cross-functional initiatives begin.

Decision makers too often view the budget as the most critical success factor for successful initiatives. They become convinced that, if they write a big enough check, and use a big enough consulting firm, the project will have all the resources necessary to be successful. Unfortunately, projects with high levels of funding usually experience major problems as companies, enabled by big budgets, try to jump from kindergarten to postgraduate school in one step. Important cross-functional initiatives rarely fail because they didn't have enough money; most large companies don't have to look too far to find projects that had large budgets and then grossly exceeded original cost estimates and at the same time accepted increasingly smaller scopes. Large enterprise projects have 70 percent failure rates, and key reasons are that their planning, governance, and implementation approaches are flawed from the start.

PRODUCTIVE GOVERNANCE HELPS PROJECTS CONTINUALLY IMPROVE

Failing transformation projects usually have unproductive governance structures. For cross-functional transformation initiatives to be successful, governance needs to be integrated at two levels: first, through an executive operating committee for the overall initiative. This group needs to be as small and as powerful as possible, with the main tasks of creating and enforcing a shared direction, removing organizational barriers as they occur, and solving problems that can't be addressed at the work-stream levels.

Second, transformation-management offices (TMOs) are often essential with complex multiproject initiatives. The TMOs work with the executive operating committees, work-stream executive sponsors, work-stream operating committees (who have the same role as the executive operating committee but at the work-stream level), and project leads. They should work with the core cross-functional stakeholders, design SP-AP sessions to accelerate and integrate business requirements, and then use those sessions to launch the implementations and detailed project plans, using an integrated cross-functional PMLC.

INTEGRATION IS REQUIRED FOR CROSS-FUNCTIONAL SUCCESS

Integrated PMLCs are critical mechanisms for successful cross-functional projects. The first steps are to establish the executive and work-stream operating committees and conduct cross-functional SP-AP sessions for work streams in order to cocreate integrated cross-functional solutions and action plans. With these complete, projects can then be implemented better and faster, avoiding the cost overruns and scope reductions that are common when using the traditional project-management approach.

The following conditions increase the success rates of important cross-functional initiatives: The vision is clear and stable (Envision); priorities are clear and actionable (Design); structure is clear and integrated, with well-defined tollgates and deadlines (Build); and accountability is clear (Activate). The velocity advantage provides important improvements to the traditional project-management approach with projects that have a high degree of cross-functional interdependence and fluidity, as shown in the table below.

The Build step is an important bridge to the fourth part of the EDBA process (the Activate step), which is the subject of the next chapter. This is where key initiatives move from plans to capabilities.

Cross-functional challenges	Solutions
People solve problems in different ways; managing this fact can take something that often works against projects and make it work for projects	Strategic Profiling insights
Cross-functional output improves dramatically when a common framework and language are shared	Envision-Design-Build-Activate process
One good collaborative session can eliminate and improve upon dozens of individual meetings	Strategic Profiling – Action Planning sessions
Organizationally integrated project and program management produces consistently better and faster outcomes	Integrated EDBA project-management life cycle (PMLC)

Key Characteristics of the "Build" Step

Build-oriented people are practical, precise, and good at turning priorities into repeatable processes; a weakness is that they can be inclined to defend the status quo.

Build characteristics include following standard processes, implementing step-by-step procedures and complex projects, assigning clear roles and responsibilities, integrating systems, using proven methods, and implementing solutions to problems.

Highlights from "Step Three – Build Deep Dive"

Strong Build capabilities help cross-functional teams productively implement priorities and create reliable infrastructures.
Executives often have low preferences in the Build area, which can create blind spots on the need for step-by-step processes.
Key Build techniques include incorporating the Pareto principle, Metcalfe's law, workflow queue elimination, constraint management, and integrated projects.
Cross-functional projects are to today's organizations what the assembly line was to the industrial age and is to factory work.
Focus, integration, and addressing blind spots in the Build step all help to lower costs and produce better, faster, and more reliable outcomes.

7

Step Four – Activate Deep Dive

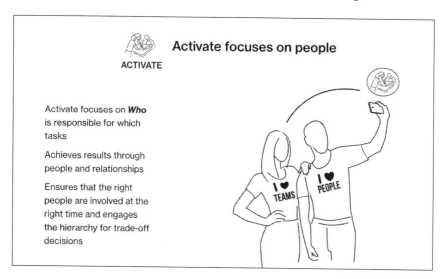

ACTIVATE

Activate focuses on people

Activate focuses on **Who** is responsible for which tasks

Achieves results through people and relationships

Ensures that the right people are involved at the right time and engages the hierarchy for trade-off decisions

I ♥ TEAMS

I ♥ PEOPLE

Scientific management has made it less fashionable to be a people person. Employees are standardized and quantitatively measured on their relative performance and value, and when employee engagement is low, the first reaction is often to measure even more by sending out more surveys. While not obvious in most investment-analyst reports, business headlines, or business textbooks, people and their interactions with one another do make all the difference. Human activation capabilities—setting a unifying tone, connecting with people's lives, supporting them when they struggle, and unleashing their spirits to achieve the firm's vision—are all essential ingredients.

* * *

To start quickly, people can work alone, but to finish quickly, they need to work together. The Activate step of the EDBA process is where the velocity advantage comes to life. The Envision step establishes a shared destination (where and why for a given time frame), Design converts the destination into a clear set of priorities (what and when), and Build establishes how to best implement critical initiatives. Activate then brings everything to life through the right people, with the right skills and motivation, at the right time.

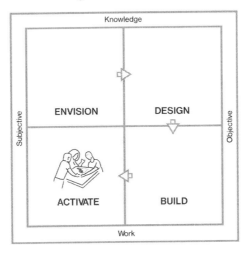

The Activate step helps to unleash human potential. Even though Activate is the fourth step in the EDBA process, it is the first thing that customers and other stakeholders see. People who get energy from the Activate area are excellent at relating to others. They have a natural ability to apply the human touch, even under difficult conditions. In companies, the Activate area includes functions such as sales, customer support, coaching, and communications. Where Design and Build folks take pride in their objectivity, Activate people solve problems subjectively and interpersonally. They are instinctive and hands-on people. They are also inconsistent at times due to their situational natures and their tendency to think out loud.

Activate-oriented people live in the moment and see complicated personal situations as a natural part of life. They are energetic and enjoy being with others. Similar to Envision, Design, and Build people, their strength can also be their weakness. Too much human spontaneity can result in actions that are off strategy, creating needless organizational confusion and resulting in unfulfilled promises.

Often fast on their feet, Activators can be good at fighting fires, which is an important skill if you're in the middle of a blaze. They are also likely to say what people want to hear in order to influence them. This can make Activate people very likable but at the same time less trusted. Successful politicians and salespeople often have strong Activate abilities.

Quantitative MBA programs and numbers-oriented functions like accounting and planning often place a low premium on the "touchy-feely" nature of Activate. Ignoring the Activate area, however, leads to suboptimal relationships and a weaker ability to influence organizational change. The Activate area can also be overemphasized. Organizations become less productive when too much coddling goes on, since this creates laissez-faire environments in which high employee morale does not help deliver strong organizational results.

This challenge has always been with us. The Xerox Palo Alto Research Center in the 1970s and 1980s is a classic example. The research center was truly remarkable for its time; it created the computer mouse, computer windows and icons, the laser printer, and the local-area network (LAN). Unfortunately, Xerox was in the copier business, and during the same time period, its copier market share dropped from 85 percent to 13 percent due to inroads from Japanese competitors. Researchers were highly motivated and creative, but their innovations were not connected to the company's business strategy. Customers increasingly bought their copiers elsewhere.

When Lou Gerstner was CEO during the turnaround of IBM in the 1990s, he didn't allow the company to follow a similar path. He insisted that the IBM Almaden Research Center in San Jose, California, focus its efforts on commercial priorities, even though this rubbed many researchers the wrong way. During his time at the helm, Gerstner reinvented IBM. He took a fallen star and successfully repositioned and reinvigorated it. I was able to meet Lou during this time. By not coddling, and by focusing on the future, he undoubtedly saved the jobs and retirements of tens of thousands of people.

Activate—when connected to the rest of the EDBA process—produces results with and through people. Two important Activate questions are, "How do employees feel about working here?" and "How do customers feel about buying here?" Like the other EDBA areas, Activate needs to be integrated—that is, who will be responsible and motivated to do what in the Activate step, linked to Build (the how), Design (the what and when), and Envision (the where and why for a given time frame).

PREFERENCES AND ABILITIES PRODUCE VELOCITY

Velocity increases when organizations activate the things that drive their people, including their preferences and abilities. Abilities are important, because skills make cross-functional success possible. Personal preferences are essential, because people spend more time on those areas that give them the most energy.

Since people are not mind readers, systematically identifying preferences and abilities through SP-AP is valuable. But we also need to motivate people through strong personal relationships. Through the Activate step, people can make the invisible more visible with employees and customers alike. Organizational outcomes happen through people, and velocity increases when their preferences and abilities are known and activated.

Every business is ultimately a people business. Attracting motivated employees—and then helping them be their best—requires constant attention, because the best people often see themselves more as free agents than as employees. With factory work, people are important as well, but employees aren't the unit of production to the same degree that they are in today's organizations. People need to be great at what they do, know what *to* do, and get a lot of personal energy from their work. Activate capabilities help to turn this potential into a sustainable organizational capability.

VALUE CREATION COMES THROUGH PEOPLE

Using a scientific-management lens, customers are segmented, measured, incentivized, and are ultimately a means to an end: achieving better internal numbers. Through a social-science lens, good numbers are a by-product of good relationships and strong value propositions. Rather than extracting value *from* customers, high-velocity companies create value *for* and *with* them. As these relationships are built, employees become more valuable themselves by improving their own understanding of customer strategies, needs, measures, business models, and expectations. In addition, working with customers at a personal level can be very energizing, since this involves moving beyond purely transactional interactions to trusted and sustainable relationships.

Customer relationships become stronger and more sustainable when they are modeled after winning alliance structures. Three key ingredients are to ensure that (1) both sides benefit, (2) they operate with a surplus mind-set, and (3) have an agreed-on exit path. In addition, organizations should:

- deliver a consistently good customer experience;
- help customers do their jobs better;
- foster community;
- skillfully communicate; and
- visibly appreciate the privilege of doing business together.

Great customer relationships foster community at every important touch point. This should happen from the boardroom to the mailroom. Customers are more loyal to people than to companies, in the same way that patients are more loyal to their doctors than to their hospitals. Creating value *with* customers benefits from a clear connection between the EDBA steps. If it is time to terminate a relationship, then don't try to hang on too long. With a proper exit, it will not be goodbye. It will be "until we meet again."

"INFORMAL" ORGANIZATIONS ARE SILENT YET POWERFUL

Every large organization has a network of formal structures and informal relationships. Formal organizational structures are guided by scientific-management principles and are easy to see on paper. Informal networks deserve special attention. Not a lot is said about informal organizations in business schools (and in business overall), yet it is informal organizations that often matter most. Sometimes you indirectly hear about them when people say things like, "It isn't *what* you know; it's *who* you know." Design-oriented people are apt to place too much faith in formal structures, whereas Activate-oriented people often appreciate (and even thrive on) informal ones.

In times of stability, informal organizations usually exist under the radar screen. They become more visible in times of change, when there are new leaders, crises, mergers, acquisitions, or restructurings. Despite the best attempts to implement objective human-resources policies and procedures, leaders with preestablished familiarity, trust, and respect play an important role during these situations.

Informal organizations are the invisible foundations of companies. All organizations begin informally, with more formalization added over time. This has always been the case. Bill Hewlett and Dave Packard started informally in a Palo Alto garage in the late 1930s and built a very large formal organization with HP. This was also true with Steve Jobs and Steve Wozniak at Apple, Bill Gates and Paul Allen at Microsoft, Larry Page and Sergey Brin at Google, and so on. Organizations are informally constructed and then formally reconstructed as they grow.

Informal organizations are powerful yet fragile. I first experienced this when I was in my early thirties during a merger between Coca-Cola Enterprises (CCE) and Johnston Coca-Cola, when the Johnston management team took over the combined company. Overnight, many of the work relationships that I and other CCE executives had developed went away. People in the formal CCE organization quickly needed to plug into, or opt out of, the Johnston network. Many well-established managers at CCE needed to effectively start over by informally gaining familiarity and earning the trust of the new management team.

I was on the other side of this equation when I was part of a turnaround team for Coca-Cola Beverages in Canada. The new CEO came in with executives who had known one another for more than a decade. When we arrived, we temporarily lived in apartments located on Elm Street in Toronto. Our choice of accommodations resulted in the unintended consequence of being referred to as the "nightmare on Elm Street," the name of a famous horror movie at the time. Eventually, as familiarity and trust developed, many new and established people came together to achieve some great things, but it took time.

The informal structure matters a lot in organizations, and it is people with strong Activate skills who navigate this often-invisible structure best, not only in the companies they work for but with customers, suppliers, and other key stakeholders as well.

EMPLOYEE COACHING IS THE GIFT THAT KEEPS ON GIVING

Personal coaching helps people be their best and get better over time. It pays off in better performance, increased job satisfaction, and decreased turnover. Done purposefully, this produces large improvements in personal productivity, especially when the rest of the EDBA process is connected. For example, coaching will not be as effective if priorities in Design or Envision statements are not clear.

Coaching is to today's companies what training was to the industrial age. Training teaches repeatable skills, whereas coaching expands human potential—helping employees and companies win in the short term as well as over the long run.

People with strong Activate skills are often good coaches. Many of today's managers, however, act more like judges or wannabe players. Good coaches combine experience, empathy, and independence to help people achieve continuous breakthroughs. This helps them accomplish personal and organizational goals better and faster, providing a catalyst for improving organizational impact and personal engagement.

When we coach clients, we try to help individuals move through four basic stages of being unaware, aware, unnatural, and natural. Before being coached, employees are often in a state of unawareness. At this stage, coaches use their experience to discover something important that the employee cannot see. Unaware employees don't know what they don't know—for instance, when managers spend too much time working "in" their functions and not enough time working "on" their functions. In this situation, they are unconscious of the fact that by working more *on* their functions, they can do a better job of developing others and also free up their time to focus on the most important problems and opportunities.

The first step of the coaching is to move individuals from unawareness to awareness. At this stage, people will know what they didn't know before. It may be uncomfortable, but it is an important growing pain. This is like learning to ride a bicycle, which isn't easy when you haven't done it before. In the "working *on* the function" example, the coach might try to help the employee improve skills such as time management and delegation.

The next stage is to help people move from being aware to making changes, even though doing so feels unnatural. At this stage, employees can do what they need to do, but it takes personal effort. Going back to the bicycle analogy, they are riding the bike but are still a little wobbly. In the "working *on* the function" example, the coach can observe and continually encourage the employee to stay the course.

The final stage is to move from being unnatural to natural. This is where competence is second nature, with the employee not even needing to think about it—much like skillfully riding a bicycle. This is the phase of personal mastery.

Unlike the disconnected nature of periodic performance reviews, good coaches stay connected and help employees build on their strengths and neutralize weaknesses. They do not try to turn weaknesses into strengths. Spending time trying to turn a weakness into a strength will almost never help an employee more than spending the same amount of time on cultivating a strength (as long as their weaknesses don't undermine their strengths).

Dr. Howard Shapiro is a world-class executive coach who has spent much of his life helping executives and their teams; he has developed and applied many insights throughout his career and at his company, Head Coach. Among these are the need to partner with leaders and to help leaders partner with one another to achieve results together. Through his work, Shapiro focuses on character, meaning getting the right results in the right way and incorporating courage, commitment, integrity, coherence, strong values, a responsibility to serve, and the integration of mind-action-heart.

Competence, another key driver in The Head Coach system, capitalizes on intelligence, empathy, self-confidence, humility, adaptability, learning and knowledge, and clarity and consistency. Linked to this is connectedness, which requires active listening, inquiry, relating, and storytelling. He also emphasizes interest in other's self-interest and recommends that his clients be "go-givers."

Interaction is an important part of this coaching approach, which emphasizes shared experiences in the service of goals and values. This benefits from information by incorporating content, context, relationships, and experiential storytelling. Then there is interdependence, which drives synergy, intimacy, reciprocity, and service. Identification, another key ingredient, is linked to connection, personal brands, and rapport. Finally, there is inspiration, including a shared vision and passion, which stimulates what already exists.

Dr. Shapiro, the creator of his company's Head Coach Way, focuses on sharing, mutual exploration and evaluation, coaching-conversation meetings, life histories, and the company's Multi-Respondent Feedback Interview (MRFI) Program, which helps others through greater service, value, relationships, and success as teams. The key, he believes, is to know what you're doing and to do what you're knowing, thus creating organizational cultures of coaching through networks of partnerships. This results in an ability to attract highly talented, high-performing individuals and to mold them into great teams as well as mentoring and coaching ongoing generations of organizational leaders.

Excellent coaches activate others. They are people experts who are able to read, motivate, and engage others. One of the most important coaching traits is the ability to ask good questions. Coaches help others achieve outcomes beyond what they would otherwise attain. In the words of Tom Landry, the legendary Dallas Cowboys coach, "A coach is someone who can tell you what you don't want to hear and make you see what you don't want to see so you can be everything you've always known you can be."

It is very powerful when coaching expands beyond a one-to-one exercise. Since value creation is a team sport, coaching is particularly powerful when it is used to activate cross-functional groups. The use of "mastermind" sessions and SP-AP are two ways to do this.

The aforementioned Napoleon Hill developed the mastermind process nearly a century ago after he interviewed many successful people of the time, including Andrew Carnegie, Thomas Edison, and Henry Ford, to discover their secrets for success. Hill found that the use of mastermind groups was a defining factor for many successful people, because the practice helped them take advantage of different knowledge bases and skills to solve problems and capitalize on opportunities.

As companies, Brand Velocity and Consequent frequently use mastermind meetings, which help participants rapidly cocreate better and more actionable answers. Mastermind conference calls are also very productive. These calls—often dealing with extremely complicated issues—usually take less than thirty minutes each. Mastermind sessions have five parts. The person calling the meeting defines the agenda:

1. the definition of success for the meeting
2. agreement on who the ultimate decision maker is
3. situation review
4. discussion points
5. necessary decision

Coaching is to people what capital is to fixed assets: it increases their output, value, and longevity. Coaching wasn't nearly as important in the industrial age, because it mostly involved machine-based, labor-supported, and repeatable work. With today's organizations, coaching is essential to help individuals and teams break through the invisible but very real barriers that prevent them from achieving their personal goals and organizational visions.

EXPERTS DON'T PERFORM; THEY CONTRIBUTE

Today's performance reviews have their roots in the industrial age. Bosses are expected to rank their people against a standard template and point out perceived strengths and weaknesses (especially weaknesses). Employees are then typically left on their own to shape up or ship out. Performance reviews often incorporate normal curves, with forced winners and losers. One flaw in using this approach with highly skilled and knowledgeable people is that experts do not perform—they *contribute*. Imagine how a performance review with Albert Einstein or Steve Jobs might have gone.

One reason that traditional performance reviews underdeliver is because employees are usually more expert in their fields than their bosses are. A better approach is for employees to reflect on what they (and the company) need to do the same and what they need to do differently. This benefits from combining 360-degree feedback with coaching for the employee, the boss, and ultimately the company overall. To this end, organizations can also benefit from Drucker's "manager's letter" process, which helps each person and manager think through, discuss, and act on the following:

1. my manager's objectives, as I see them
2. my objectives, as I see them

3. performance standards that I believe apply to me
4. how I will achieve my goals
5. specific steps I will take and resources I will need
6. things that the company and my manager do that help me
7. things that the company and my manager do that hinder me

People in today's "neural" organizations become more productive when there is less judging and more coaching, with fewer reviews and greater personal reflection as well as more direction and inspiration. Moving the focus from personal performance to organizational contribution and outcomes increases velocity.

DELIBERATE FACILITATION OUTPERFORMS COMMAND AND CONTROL

Something that I learned as a consultant that I did not understand well as a business executive was that command and control was largely delusional. When I led large organizations, employees and vendors would positively nod their heads when I asked them to work on things. It often turned out that they really didn't know what I was asking for, and too frequently I didn't truly know, either. We commonly see this same issue in facilitated cross-functional sessions, when teams and their leaders work together to create Envision statements and action plans for key initiatives.

This command-and-control delusion, combined with the incorrect belief that cross-functional teams can collaborate productively on contentious issues without facilitation, often make executives believe their organizations are changing faster than they really are. Then, many months later, they can't believe how little progress has been made. Facilitated cross-functional solutions produce much better and faster outcomes. With cross-functional work, to increase velocity, command and control should be replaced by facilitated collaboration using a shared framework, language, and process.

Cross-functional initiatives commonly struggle when the initial requirements are not cocreated by the right people in an integrated way. There are great benefits from establishing a shared vision and time frame and a clear set of priorities. With complicated issues, facilitated planning up front saves a lot of time, money, and aggravation over the longer term. This improves the speed and quality of organizational change efforts by building in the necessary support up front.

Consulting firms commonly try to use overly detailed processes and stand-alone change-management teams to compensate for not being able to get the right people involved at the right time. In practice, an ounce of hierarchical involvement and cross-functional collaboration is worth a pound of external change management. The productive use of SP-AP is one way to achieve this, in conjunction with leading-edge thinking. One client connected the dots using some of the principles of Harvard's John Kotter, in this way.

Change Management	SP-AP Process
Establish urgency with the right people	Conduct SP-AP sessions with the right people and sponsors
Have a shared vision	Cocreate a single Envision statement and integrated plan
Empower people	Activate the EDBA process through the right people at the right time
Create wins and build momentum	Implement milestones using the EDBA project-management life cycle

EMOTIONS STRENGTHEN COMMUNICATIONS

Through strengths in the Activate area, organizations can more successfully unleash their human potential through emotional connection and productive communications. Companies often struggle with this. If people consider emotions at all, they apologize for them as soft skills or touchy-feely stuff. Emotions, though, connect us. They increase energy and productivity. Feelings that produce good results include the following:

- the desire to win
- the achievement of something worthwhile
- a sense of personal power
- approval and acceptance
- recognition

People have a deep need for appreciation, and neglect can be more damaging than abuse. If you really want to honor someone, ask for the person's help. Great leaders lead with their heads *and* their hearts, and in difficult times, emotional resistance can often be overcome by positive emotions. Optimism, hope, faith, courage, ambition, determination, self-confidence, and self-worth all activate the human spirit and help people achieve better and faster organizational outcomes.

Velocity increases when communications are integrated with strong emotional connections, understanding that people process information differently. Where a Design-oriented person might be blunt, an Activate-oriented person may be overly nice. Fortunately, it's possible to combine the blunt facts of Design with the personal sensitivity of Activate. This is called tact, which is the emotional equivalent of when a nurse gives a patient a shot without it hurting too much.

Communications are often a social negotiation in companies. When there is the need for organizational change, effective communications help to connect the dots between where you've been, where you are now, and where you intend to go, because if something doesn't fit with the past, it will often be discarded or misread. Since adults learn by reconstructing their experiences, skillfully communicating a transition from the past to the future is usually very effective.

Great communicators ask excellent questions and stick to a single theme. They help people share their own knowledge and beliefs. They are also able to clearly articulate—linked to a clear Envision statement—what needs to stay the same, what needs to change, the steps that are required, and the progress that has already been made. They use clear communication strategies to help people achieve organizational visions.

As with the rest of EDBA, less is also more in the Activate area. Short-term memory is limited to four or five items. Three is better. If you have more than five points, people will not remember any of them. It is important to be consistent; even better is if you can make people feel genuinely wanted and loved, inspiring them to achieve something as part of the group that they can't achieve alone.

People with strong activate skills are at their best when they can set an inspiring tone, connect with people's lives, support others when they struggle, provide levity in difficult times, and motivate key stakeholders to achieve the firm's vision.

Key Characteristics of the "Activate" Step

Activate-oriented people solve problems through strong personal relationships; a weakness is that they can find it difficult to get into the details and follow rules.

Activate characteristics include building strong personal relationships, working in teams, coaching and emotionally supporting others, relating to people, communicating strategically, and being spontaneous.

Highlights from "Step Four – Activate Deep Dive"

The Activate area helps bring outcomes to life – with people who have the right skills and motivation at the right time.

Understanding people's preferences and priorities helps organizations unleash human potential in the Activate step.

Coaching and mentoring are important ingredients to help people be their best. They pay off in better performance, increased job satisfaction, and decreased turnover.

Effective leaders use clear, consistent, and emotionally engaging communications to achieve organizational visions.

Recognition, the desire to win, the achievement of something worthwhile, increased personal power, and approval and acceptance are important traits to communicate and cultivate.

8

How to Make Velocity Your Brand

Big companies don't beat small ones; fast companies beat slow ones. It is easy to have speed without direction. It's also easy to have direction without speed. It is the combination of speed and direction that determines success. Velocity defines companies, products, and services as well as their relative positions in the marketplace. This book shows how, in today's rapidly changing world, velocity can be built into every company's genetic code: corporately, divisionally, functionally, and through every cross-functional initiative. It shows how organizations can systematically implement and achieve the velocity advantage, one project at a time. If your company, organization, or team is equal in all other respects, then velocity will be your winning differentiator. The velocity advantage will ultimately define who you are today and who you will become.

* * *

Twenty years ago, after Brand Velocity was founded, I wrote that the enterprise itself was a company's most valuable brand. This was soon after I left Coke, at a time when the Coca-Cola brand was indisputably the most valuable in the world. I had discovered that, in most companies, the secret to building strong and sustainable brands was a little like asking the royal family how to get rich. How would they know? They've always been rich. As a client once told me, "today's employees sometimes wake up on third base and think they hit a triple." Most large companies were well established before current management arrived, and they became successful because they were fast at implementing at least one significant competitive advantage. Brands are not competitive advantages—they are the result of them.

FOUR BRAND MYTHS

Myth #1: *Brands are durable assets.* Brand equity is the result—not the source—of competitive advantage, requiring a winning business model, the ability to move with speed and direction, and the capability to systematically run and change the company's operations at the same time.

Myth #2: *Brands can command premium prices.* It is not the brand, but competitive advantage that can command premium prices. If a product or service offering is overpriced relative to its competitive advantage, then brand equity will decline, regardless of its market position.

Myth #3: *Brand loyalty is achievable over the long term.* Brand preference, not brand loyalty, is the better goal, because people ultimately buy their best alternatives; it is competitive advantage that creates these advantages. Velocity is the mechanism for achieving and sustaining it.

Myth #4: *Marketing builds brands.* The best allocation of resources and competitive advantages build brands. Sometimes a brand's problem is marketing, but the constraint is often some other part of the company's business or business model. Most notably, trying to be all things to all people and doing the wrong things with excellence.

IDENTITY PRECEDES IMAGE

Image is the consequence of identity. It's similar to the difference between progress and purpose. Purpose drives progress in the same way that identity determines image. Brands are not images to be manipulated; they are paychecks to be earned, through a winning business model, with continuous improvements via high-velocity, cross-functional initiatives. A great brand is an organizational promise that's delivered on through continuously improving capabilities. This is the heartbeat of superior and sustainable brand equity.

Great brands are the result of much more than great marketing. While a brand's image does need to consistently break through the clutter, brands can never have a consistently clear image if their companies don't have velocity. To increase velocity, brands require a clear strategic focus (Envision), a well-defined product/service offering (Design), an effective operating infrastructure (Build), and unique organizational capabilities (Activate). They require a clear direction that customers can see, a product and service offering that customers prefer, an operating infrastructure that they can trust, and meaningful human relationships that they feel excited about.

Brands have evolved from trademarks to ecosystems and from images to delivered promises. Velocity has become the essential ingredient of all brands; it drives the relative performance of products and services and in some cases actually defines them. Amazon improved faster than brick-and-mortar retailers; Apple improved faster than Microsoft, Nokia, and

Sony; and Uber moved faster than conventional transportation services. Winning requires speed and direction. A defining characteristic of high-flying brands is that they are fast yet intentional. The disrupters are never slow. The disrupted are always slow.

Companies with greater velocity have become the new elite. Without velocity, Apple would be known for the Mac, Google for Internet searching, and Amazon for books. They all moved with greater speed and direction than their competitors, and their customers and the stock market rewarded them for it. If these companies get disrupted, they will be beaten for the same reason.

Brands are a lagging—not a leading—indicator of value creation, with velocity as the most sustainable source of competitive advantage. This was a new idea when Brand Velocity was founded, yet now it is a statement of the obvious. The brands of people, products, services, and companies alike are either tarnished or polished by their speed and direction.

The velocity advantage is the ultimate competitive weapon for today's companies. Its absence makes companies uncompetitive and employees disengaged. Companies with low velocity rarely have an absence of activity, but they almost always lack vibrancy and meaningful change. Velocity can be systematically increased on a company-wide basis by applying the recommendations in this book. Although not every idea discussed in this book will apply to every company, this chapter provides a few thought starters for achieving superior reputations and results in today's marketplace.

YOU CAN MAKE VELOCITY YOUR BRAND IN SEVERAL WAYS

The velocity-advantage brand architecture shows ten ways to increase velocity, all of which can be done better and faster by using the Envision-Design-Build-Activate (EDBA) process, Strategic Profiling–Action Planning (SP-AP), and the EDBA project-management life cycle (PMLC).

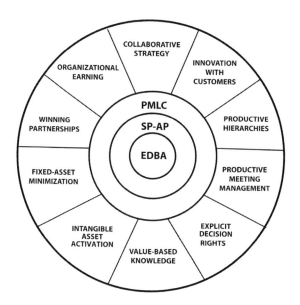

Capitalize on the power of collaborative strategy

Adopting the *Playing to Win* strategy process (discussed in chapters 3 and 4) and incorporating the recommendations in this book will help to increase velocity at the corporate, divisional, and functional levels. Doing this helps to effectively and efficiently make important choices to cocreate winning aspirations, define where you will play and how you will win, identify the capabilities you need, and determine the management systems necessary for success. This strategy process helps get the right people in the same room to develop plans that are both better and more actionable.

Innovate with customers

In the industrial age, companies could successfully innovate internally and roll out new products and services to largely captive markets. Today's companies need to profitably sell to tailored markets (sometimes markets of one person). This has been a difficult shift for many established firms to make. In the "old days," companies could sell a few core brands that produced high volumes and profits. Large blocks of advertising then helped these companies control the dialogue in the marketplace and kept new entrants at bay. Today, established companies have bimodal sales curves, where they face simultaneous pressures on two ends of an ever-widening spectrum. High-volume products get pressure on price, while new entrants introduce niche products faster and more profitably. Marketing and advertising have been redefined, and barriers to entry have shrunk.

This sea change for established companies puts gross-profit pressure on traditional brands and requires high investments in a growing number of new products. Although new products can sometimes generate higher gross margins per sale, their total contribution is usually smaller and riskier, with many "one-year wonders." New products are introduced with great internal fanfare and then die on the vine due to the lack of sustainable interest.

This makes innovating with customers a safer and more productive way to transform. Fortunately for today's companies, customer relationships are often a competitive advantage in established firms. Working *with* customers through joint pilots is an excellent way to capitalize on this opportunity.

To achieve a velocity advantage, innovation efforts should adopt a systematic approach with strategic customers and place a high priority on innovating infrastructures. The winners will systematically do a better job of managing and exceeding customer expectations, show a genuine interest in the customer's customer, act with integrity, and communicate with clarity.

Intentionally activate your hierarchy

We have known the pros and cons of organizational hierarchies for generations. The educator Dr. Laurence Peter established the notion of "hierarchiology" in the late 1960s. He conducted hundreds of studies and found that employees often rose to their "levels of incompetence." He saw that people who did their jobs well were promoted into jobs in which they could no longer perform. This became known as the "Peter principle." During his research, Peter found that good followers often didn't become good leaders, and strong leaders were frequently not good conformers.

The Peter principle's first commandment is that companies preserve their hierarchies at any cost. It was in this context that he coined the term "unproductivity." He found that this problem contributed to Parkinson's law, an idea that had been proposed a decade earlier by Cyril Parkinson. Parkinson found that left unmanaged staff continually grow and that work tends to expand to fill the allotted time to do it in, concluding that too few can in fact accomplish more than too many.

As staff expands, these smart and hardworking people want to be active and work on things that they find interesting. Due to the interdependent nature of today's work, they usually can't do this without also enlisting the time of others. This often creates a lot of activity with very little strategically relevant output. This wasted effort is usually invisible but costly. Organizations don't typically have good mechanisms in place for individuals to pay a personal price when they increase staff-related expenses. To the contrary, the size of someone's organization usually correlates to his or her prestige. This is one reason why staff expansion requires constant vigilance.

Even though hierarchies have their flaws, well-designed ones are needed to improve velocity. Working without a well-defined organizational decision-structure is the most unproductive situation of all. Clearly constructed hierarchies are a good thing, even though they will try to preserve themselves, accumulate staff, and produce some degree of incompetence up the chain of command. Productive decision making and effective resource allocation depend on them.

Coordinating activities and escalating issues both increase velocity. The social scientist and medical doctor Elliott Jaques made some important discoveries about this. First, he found that it was critical for managers to actively coordinate the activities of their employees so that the employees don't duplicate their efforts or work on conflicting activities. Second, he found that managers should not hire their own direct reports because they will be inclined to hire people who are too much like themselves and who will pose no future threat.

Coordinating functional priorities through integrated executive teams increases velocity, because improving one part of the company may not improve the performance of the company overall. A world-class manufacturing organization will not necessarily translate into a world-class company. This coordination requires constant vigilance, because functional tribes have a propensity to be inwardly focused and to create strong "we/them" lines. When a company lacks deliberate coordination, employees will identify more with their functional specialty and priorities than with the organization overall. This institutionally reduces velocity when market changes occur that require resources to be reallocated. By proactively and systematically managing the hierarchy, velocity will improve for top management, frontline employees, the organization overall, and—most important—customers.

Replace meeting with working

Over time, the number of meetings has increased as companies have become more fragmented and calendars have gotten more automated. More than two generations of managers now seem to accept that because they are busy, they are productive (and meetings make people busy). This produces mountains of wasted effort every minute of every day.

I often hear managers talk about their "good" meetings, but the test of a good meeting is, what's different because of it? Drucker used to say to his clients, "Don't tell me you had a great meeting with me. What will you do different on Monday?" Productive meetings end with trade-off decisions and immediate actions, with the ultimate decision maker present. If the objective isn't to make a decision that changes something, then that meeting may well be unnecessary.

When I was at Coke, I was asked to lead the turnaround of a $1 billion technology project. Since the project was already under way, I inherited my predecessor's calendar. Meetings had been systematically set up with key stakeholders, which included more than a hundred executives around the world. When I dismantled the meeting calendar, two positive things happened. First, I had time to think and focus. Second, when I requested a meeting, it was urgent *and* important, and the executives I needed decisions from were always willing to get together on short notice for those types of meetings.

Since then, I have worked on many large turnarounds and have consistently found governance structures to be overengineered in these troubled situations. In an attempt to be inclusive, governance meetings too often focus on sharing information and building consensus instead of making choices. With large cross-functional initiatives, this results in scope creep, time delays, and cost overruns. For important projects to function well, there should be fewer cooks in the kitchen and fewer automatically scheduled meetings.

In addition to having too many meetings, striving for alignment is a common organizational "head fake." Alignment sounds like something that is good, but it's often code for "let's get along as tribes." For tribes to get along, though, no one can make a trade-off that positively affects one tribe at the expense of another. Yet this is exactly what is necessary to increase velocity in a changing environment.

Make decision rights explicit

Decision rights are akin to property rights, and we've known how to manage property rights for a couple of centuries. The economist Adam Smith's thoughts on property rights have helped increase wealth and improve living standards since the late 1700s. He was the first to see that property rights were important to the competitiveness of nations and the wealth of their citizens. In companies, decision rights are managed through policies, budgets, organization charts, formal power, and informal influence.

These rights need to adapt to ever-changing environments. With industrialized work, last year's decision rights will usually work pretty well the year after. With organizational work, however, if these decision rights cannot adjust, then the past will get overfunded, and the future will be underfunded.

Actively managing decision rights is essential to organizational success and sustainability. Rather than stopping what is no longer needed and reinvesting in the future, executives often try to play it safe and just tighten their belts across the board. In the same way that squeezing into tighter pants doesn't make us more fit, belt-tightening doesn't increase a company's competitiveness. Decision rights need to mirror the company's vision; this requires very clear "not-to-do" lists for work that is not on strategy. We shouldn't try to more efficiently do things that shouldn't be done at all.

Large companies can learn from start-ups when it comes to decision rights, because the intentions of successful new companies are usually clear, and their resources are often constrained. Their resulting decision-making capabilities make it possible for start-ups to compete with much bigger firms, despite the fact that bigger firms have more resources and more established reputations.

Apply knowledge through a valuation lens

Knowledge is infinitely scalable, but it has a short shelf life. Even though it is an intangible asset, knowledge should be managed in the same way that financial professionals manage fixed assets. The key is to manage the company's knowledge like a portfolio of investments. From a valuation perspective, this is analogous to owning "pure plays" rather than lower-valued conglomerates. This also applies to project selection. Choosing low-value projects is like buying companies in lower-valued industries. Eventually, they will bring down the overall valuation.

Since experts are today's organizational means of production, valuation principles can help companies direct their knowledge to the highest-value areas. Just like with fixed assets and other investments, knowledge that increases profitable growth is the best value driver. After profitable growth, sustainable expense improvements are the second-best value drivers. One-time benefits are the least valuable.

To improve your velocity advantage, review how you are investing your human capital from an asset-allocation perspective. Measure how much of your human capital and project portfolio are focused on profitable growth and sustainable operating-profit increases versus one-time improvements and administration. If you don't like what you see, then you should strategically reinvest.

Activate your intangible assets

From a valuation perspective, fixed assets such as buildings and machinery are usually a company's lowest-value holdings. The most valuable assets are usually intangibles such as brands, intellectual property, contracts, customer relationships, and key people.

Since the people, products, and services that can increase profitable revenue are a company's most valuable assets, be cautious about making investments in nonrevenue-producing assets and guard against spending too much associated management time with them. Consider how you would run your company if you could have no fixed assets at all. This idea revolutionized the hotel industry when Marriott transformed itself from a hotel owner to a hotel-management company. Today, managing hotels this way is the industry standard, with most hotel brands focusing on their secret sauce and using external partners to finance their physical locations. This has been taken a step further with Airbnb, the online marketplace and hospitality service. The company does not own any lodging; it is merely a broker and receives service fees.

Managing with an intangible-asset mind-set can help organizations take full advantage of the nearly unlimited scalability of knowledge (i.e., companies can use knowledge and still keep it). Using this mind-set can also help executives think more strategically about their noncore activities. For example, it is curious why companies usually don't mind outsourcing their advertising to get the best ideas, yet they hold on to their in-house accounting shops and supply chains as if they were the crown jewels.

With fixed assets, managing economic profit (which calculates a company's net profit after subtracting a capital charge) helps companies identify things that look like they are earning money on the income statement but are actually destroying value because of their asset intensity. An equivalent measure for organizational work should penalize activities that seem accretive on the surface but have a significant opportunity cost when management's time is factored in. Try looking at where you spend your time and then compare that to where the greatest value drivers for your company are located. Most managers will find opportunities for improvement.

One fixed asset in transition is the traditional office. How the traditional-virtual office equation will play out is unclear, but to improve productivity in the twenty-first century in the same way that industrialized work improved in the twentieth century, reinventing the nine-to-five office model will be a game changer for several reasons. First, in the global economy, companies are competing with one another around the clock. Second, competition for the best minds (wherever they choose to live) continues to increase in significance because *great* people produce substantially more than *good* ones. Finally, with the lowest competitive barriers to entry in commercial history, companies now need experts more than experts need particular companies.

Most companies cannot be 100 percent traditional or 100 percent virtual. Organizations need to be traditional enough to produce a well-functioning organization yet virtual enough to compete anywhere in the world at any time—with as few fixed assets as possible. Most organizations still have a long way to go, and many established companies are not in a good place. They've taken the most advanced IT tools ever created and layered them on top of their old infrastructures. They've added all the costs of being virtual on top of all the costs of being traditional.

There will always be people who require an office, and there's no good substitute for face-to-face interaction when collaboration and change management are required. Just as the number of farms fell dramatically as farming became more productive, and the number of manufacturing plants fell during the industrial age, the number of offices required to support today's and tomorrow's work will inevitably decline as well, thus reducing the need for fixed assets, long commutes, frequent relocations, and inflexible work hours.

Invest in a future with fewer fixed assets

The capital budgets of established companies are usually, by their very nature, highly correlated to their historic business models, and they focus on the infrastructure that is credited for their success. As a result, investments in the future are starved through this institutionalization of previous spending levels. One way to become more efficient is to consolidate infrastructures, but if not careful, this can calcify yesterday's business models even more.

Given that the executives who run companies have often been there for years, it is natural to want to build on the company's past. It's therefore natural that the first response is to improve or consolidate old structures without putting in enough effort in trying to disrupt the current asset base using different future-oriented business models. Since fixed assets usually create the least value, one way to move beyond the current state is to investigate how to grow your business without fixed assets—in the same way that a start-up company would try to disrupt an industry.

Large firms in established industries own and manage billions of dollars of fixed assets, yet they are often not world-class at managing these assets. It is worth asking whether companies are investing too much in things that they should not be managing internally. Perhaps a captive third party with specialized skills and a better capital structure would be a better answer.

In many respects, this is what Sam Ginn did when he incubated AirTouch inside the Pacific Telesis organization. It is how Apple got into the music business, how Uber got into the delivery business, how numerous companies have leveraged the cloud infrastructures of Amazon, Microsoft, and Google, and so on.

Win with the best partnerships

Commercial success can be enhanced by integrating better internal *and* external knowledge and relationships. Internally, working better across functions helps increase velocity; externally, doing so helps to be able to work more productively with the best business partners. This is how major business-to-business software companies were able to grow so rapidly, including Microsoft, SAP, Oracle, Salesforce, and others.

One opportunity—linked to the company's vision—is to control core functions internally and achieve noncore work through external partners. Many companies have attempted large-scale outsourcing to do this, but because they haven't done this holistically or managed it effectively, outsourcing has often underdelivered. These efforts have too often been done in a piecemeal way, wrongly focused too much on lower blended hourly rates, or have been Hail Mary passes to manage short-term earnings.

External sourcing can increase velocity if the company's ecosystem is consistent with its vision. Key questions to answer are, "Where do we own our noncore processes, and where do noncore processes own us by requiring too much capital and management time?" Consider rethinking how the pieces fit together, including accounting processes, IT and logistics infrastructure, human-resources administration, and procurement. Regardless of the answer, these higher-velocity ecosystems should share a common framework, language, and process.

If partnerships can't be managed strategically, then keeping everything internal may be the best option. Alliances should help companies improve their core business. Otherwise, they will become management distractions and will waste dollars while trying to save pennies.

Turn learning into earning

The idea of creating learning organizations emerged more than twenty-five years ago. While concepts like organizational learning and system dynamics were and are interesting, learning needs to translate into faster outcomes—and most established companies struggle to do this effectively. If learning alone resulted in better and faster outcomes, then universities would be the most productive institutions on earth. Their costs have consistently outpaced inflation, however, which is an irrefutable sign of unproductivity. In companies, learning needs to turn into earning, which requires velocity.

Earning organizations can be judged by their ability to win with customers. The promise of the velocity advantage is to do this more systematically by building better, faster, more humane, and more productive organizations—ones that people want to be part of and do business with. Companies that encourage great people to join, stay, and do the best work of their lives. They need to generate excellent returns for customers, employees, communities, and shareholders alike. Focusing only on the shareholder, rather than on employees and customers, is like focusing on the pulse rate rather than the heart that produces it.

The idea that learning needs to translate into earning is not new. Founders like Walmart's Sam Walton, McDonald's Ray Kroc, and Microsoft's Bill Gates never stopped learning from their customers, competitors, and suppliers as their companies grew to the point of dominance. Their learning had a purpose. They converted learning into earning, thereby providing great value for their customers while generating enormous wealth for the company's owners at the same time.

Having an organizational ability to rapidly and systematically convert learning into earning will produce sustainable competitive advantages. This, in a nutshell, is at the heart of optimizing neurons and implementing the velocity advantage. Employee engagement will improve as a by-product, because most people like to win and don't like to work in organizations where it is difficult to make a difference.

Join the velocity-advantage movement

The hardest business models to change are those that have worked for us in the past. Successful practices eventually become constrained, and when this happens, it is hard to give up the tried and true. The approach that improved productivity fifty-fold in the twentieth century is constrained. It is not working for established companies today, nor will it work in the future.

This book was written to help people systematically increase their velocity and, in the process, achieve goals better, faster, and with greater engagement. We already know the outcome of continuing to do what we've been doing using traditional practices: disengaged employees, wasted effort, and unproductive outcomes. In the same way that a butterfly is much more than an improved caterpillar, we need to undergo a metamorphosis by leaving scientific management behind and embracing the power of a more effective, efficient, and collaborative way of working, all linked to the power of better and faster cross-functional initiatives.

We live in a challenging yet exciting time. The good news is that by making velocity our brand—and adopting the ideas in this book—we can achieve better performance *from* our companies, build more fun *into* them, and ultimately create a better society for all.

Highlights from "How to Make Velocity Your Brand"
Velocity is the most sustainable source of competitive advantage. It systematically operationalizes differentiation and cost advantages.
Working with customers to innovate helps improve speed, reduce risk, and achieve better outcomes.
Systematically improving velocity is the way of the future. The absence of velocity makes companies uncompetitive and strangles the life out of employees.
We need to manage differently, through the better uses of strategy, hierarchy, decision making, collaboration, and valuation-based knowledge investments.
The velocity advantage will help you achieve better performance from and build more fun into your company and will create a better society for all.

Measure Your Knowledge

If you're interested in testing your knowledge on what you've read in *The Velocity Advantage*, please review the following questions. The answers are available at www.brandvelocity.com.

1. **The purpose of the book *The Velocity Advantage* is:**
   a. to explain why traditional scientific-management techniques fail to work well in knowledge-based organizations;
   b. to introduce a management model and process for improving the speed and direction of organizational work (work that is invisible, interdependent, and ever changing);
   c. to explain how to understand and apply the Envision-Design-Build-Activate (EDBA) model and process, Strategic Profiling—Action Planning (SP-AP), and the project-management life cycle (PMLC);
   d. all of the above.

2. **What question does "Envision" answer in EDBA?**
   a. Where do we intend to go, why, and in what time frame?
   b. What priorities need to happen, and when?
   c. How can we best implement the most important priorities?
   d. Who will best be able to do an implementation?

3. **What question does "Design" answer in EDBA?**

    a. Where do we intend to go, why, in what time frame?

    b. What priorities need to happen, and when?

    c. How can we best implement the most important priorities?

    d. Who will best be able to do an implementation?

4. **What question does "Build" answer in EDBA?**

    a. Where do we intend to go, why, and in what time frame?

    b. What priorities need to happen, and when?

    c. How can we best implement the most important priorities?

    d. Who will best be able to do an implementation?

5. **What question does "Activate" answer in EDBA?**

    a. Where do we intend to go, why, and in what time frame?

    b. What priorities need to happen, and when?

    c. How can we best implement the most important priorities?

    d. Who will best be able to do an implementation?

6. **Pick the characteristic that is not part of Envision:**

    a. relating to people

    b. thinking strategically

    c. creating a visionary destination

    d. brainstorming new ideas

7. **Pick the characteristic that is not part of Design:**

    a. engaging in detailed planning

    b. being spontaneous

    c. establishing clear measures

    d. being objective

8. **Pick the characteristic that is not part of Build:**
   a. following standard processes
   b. implementing step-by-step procedures
   c. establishing detailed objectives
   d. using proven methods

9. **Pick the characteristic that is not part of Activate:**
   a. building strong relationships
   b. coaching others
   c. being spontaneous
   d. being creative

10. **The best sequence to manage work is:**
    a. Envision, Activate, Design, Build
    b. Design, Envision, Build, Activate
    c. Envision, Design, Build, Activate
    d. Build, Activate, Envision, Design

11. **Which is not an attribute of Strategic Profiling?**
    a. It judges whether someone is suitable for a specific job.
    b. It helps people visualize their preferences and abilities.
    c. It highlights potential team blind spots.
    d. It helps people internalize the EDBA framework.

12. **This is not a good application for SP-AP:**
    a. productively cocreating integrated cross-functional initiatives;
    b. helping teams solve important issues better and faster;
    c. helping a key constituency get a wayward project on track;
    d. substituting SP-AP for a brainstorming session without having an objective.

13. Which is not true of the EDBA project-management life cycle (PMLC)?

a. It is the most detailed approach in the industry.
b. It productively operationalizes the output from SP-AP sessions.
c. It helps sustain the EDBA language, model, and thought process.
d. It integrates cross-functional stakeholders at the right time.

14. Every Strategic Profile has a unique productivity path.

a. True
b. False

15. What is considered most important in Strategic Profiling?

a. abilities
b. preferences

16. Profiles that are more holistic tend to have:

a. better results;
b. gap issues;
c. sequence opportunities;
d. neither gap nor sequence opportunities.

17. Profiles that are more skewed tend to have:

a. better results;
b. gap issues;
c. sequence opportunities;
d. gap and sequence opportunities.

18. **To increase velocity, people with the "Holistic Worker" EDBA profile should:**

    a. ensure that they continually follow the EDBA sequence;
    b. help coach others who have a gap in their EDBA sequence;
    c. be in charge, since they have all areas covered;
    d. work independently, since there is no obvious need for others.

19. **If someone is a "Strategic Connector" (Envision/ Activate), then:**

    a. The person may have a significant blind spot in Design and Build.
    b. He or she is likely to jump to an immediate answer.
    c. He or she can follow the EDBA process flawlessly.
    d. All of the above.

20. **Many teams have holistic SPs, which means that:**

    a. Teams will work well naturally because they have all bases covered.
    b. Improved EDBA sequence is often the biggest productivity driver.
    c. The right skills are present for success.
    d. The team is likely to get along well.

21. **The equation for the velocity advantage (VA) is:**

    a. EDBA = VA
    b. SP-AP = VA
    c. PMLC = VA
    d. EDBA + SP-AP + PMLC = VA

22. The velocity advantage will not achieve:
    a. a common language, framework, and process for key stakeholders;
    b. the potential to significantly improve speed and direction;
    c. a process to systematically improve cross-functional results;
    d. guaranteed success.

23. SP-AP should be used for improving strategy work.
    a. True
    b. False

24. SP-AP should be used when a new leader or team member joins the group.
    a. True
    b. False

25. SP-AP should be used when launching key initiatives.
    a. True
    b. False

26. SP-AP should be used to set functional and cross-functional priorities.
    a. True
    b. False

27. SP-AP should be used to more rapidly address urgent issues.
    a. True
    b. False

28. The velocity advantage should result in people being:
    a. better leaders;
    b. more focused on outcomes;
    c. better team players;
    d. all of the above.

29. Good Envision statements don't require a clear purpose or time frame.
    a. True
    b. False

30. The Design step turns the Envision statement into a clear set of priorities.
    a. True
    b. False

31. Numbers are ultimately the destination.
    a. True
    b. False

32. Build capabilities are a common blind spot in today's organizations.
    a. True
    b. False

33. "Less is more" is a velocity-advantage-guiding principle.
    a. True
    b. False

34. Queue reduction, the 80/20 rule, and the *N* formula are most important for this step:
    a. Envision
    b. Design
    c. Build
    d. Activate

35. To improve velocity (speed and direction):
    a. Unproductive practices should be stopped.
    b. Areas of strength should be built upon.
    c. New activities should be started.
    d. All of the above apply.

36. This is to the knowledge age what the assembly line was to the industrial age:
    a. knowledge-work productivity;
    b. cross-functional projects;
    c. information systems;
    d. human achievement.

37. Coaching is to knowledge work what training is to manual work.
    a. True
    b. False

38. Emotionally based communication(s) that produce better results in the Activate step lead to:
    a. the desire to win;
    b. approval and acceptance;
    c. recognition;
    d. all of the above.

39. Strong Activate capabilities benefit from the right people with the right skills and motivation at the right time, linked to Envision, Design, and Build.
    a. True
    b. False

40. You should embrace the velocity advantage to achieve better performance from your company, build more fun into it, and create a better society for all.

    a. True
    b. False

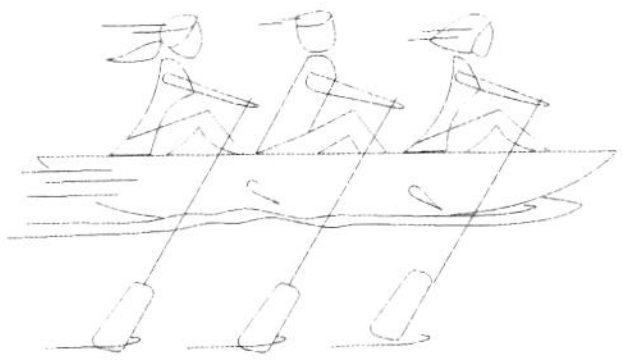

Glossary

Activate: The fourth step of the knowledge-work productivity system; it has a "subjective work" orientation and focuses on *who* should be responsible for which tasks.

analysis paralysis: The state of overanalyzing (or overthinking) a situation so that a decision or action is never taken, in effect paralyzing the outcome.

balance sheet: A financial report that tracks a company's assets and liabilities. Similar to owning a house, the difference between the value of the assets and the liabilities is equity.

board of directors: Governs organizations for owners and other stakeholders by choosing the CEO, approving strategic plans and budgets, and overseeing audits and compensation.

boiling the ocean: The common application of this phrase is to take on an overly large and potentially impossible task given the reality of your resources. The phrase implies a lack of connectivity to reality.

Brand Velocity: A consulting firm that specializes in solving issues and implementing solutions in companies using its knowledge-work productivity expertise.

Build: The third step of the knowledge-work productivity system; it has an "objective work" orientation and is focused on *how* work can best be done.

BV: Abbreviation for Brand Velocity.

capital investments: Money that companies spend on purchasing or creating assets that have long lives, including buildings, trucks, and large information systems.

CEO: Chief executive officer. The top job in a company. The CEO is responsible for the firm's strategy, performance, shareholders, employees, and other key stakeholders.

CFO: Chief financial officer. Oversees the financial affairs of a company. The CFO is responsible for the company's accounting, tax, treasury, and investor relations.

CIO: Chief information officer. Responsible for overseeing computer-related operations in companies, including software, hardware, networks, and data security. In some cases, "CIO" also refers to a chief investment officer.

cognitive mapping: A modeling technique for drawing diagrams of (and making connections between) the mental models that individuals and groups possess on specific topics.

competency trap: Occurs when continuing favorable performance with an inferior procedure leads an organization to accumulate more experience with it, thus avoiding experience with a superior procedure or keeping such experience at a low level.

Consequent: Consulting firm owned by Brand Velocity Inc.

contingency process: A method that helps the board, executive management, project team, consulting systems integrator, and software owner to manage accelerated projects.

COO: Chief operating officer. The top operating job of a company. The COO is responsible for the day-to-day performance of the company's business units.

cybernetic hierarchy: The sociologist Talcott Parsons's application of cybernetics to social systems through his general theory of action, tied to adaptation, goals, integration, and motivation.

cybernetic management: A subjective and objective process to manage knowledge-work productivity using the EDBA knowledge-work productivity system.

cybernetics: The science of relationships, control, and organization. It was developed by mathematician Norbert Wiener in 1948 to facilitate self-steering.

Design: The second step of the knowledge-work productivity system; it has an "objective knowledge" orientation and is focused on *what* needs to be done *when*.

detached engagement: A leadership approach that combines a consistent and unemotional focus on the overall vision and problem solving with a sense of urgency about day-to-day goals.

economic profit: The profit that a company generates, less a charge for the assets that it takes to generate the profit (since the firm's asset investment is an opportunity cost).

economic value added: The change in economic profit from year to year.

EDBA: The abbreviation for Envision, Design, Build, Activate, which is the basis for the velocity advantage model in this book.

enterprise projects: Large initiatives that benefit from the knowledge-work productivity system and independent facilitation to manage constraints and improve speed and quality.

entrepreneur: An opportunistic leader who manages the risks and rewards associated with being commercially successful on one hand and going out of business on the other.

Envision: The first step of the knowledge-work productivity system; it has a "subjective knowledge" orientation and is focused on *where* the company intends to go and *why*.

escalation: In organizational work this means escalating the need to solve a problem or make a decision to someone with more power in the hierarchy.

executive operating committee: executive decision-making and problem-solving governance teams that are part of the velocity-advantage project-management life cycle (PMLC) at both the overall and work-stream levels.

financial assets: Companies have liquid assets (such as cash) and fixed assets (such as buildings). Intangible assets (such as intellectual property) are only tracked on the balance sheet if money has been paid for them.

free cash flow: The money a company generates after all of its cash expenses have been factored in. It is similar to the money left over from your paycheck after all bills are paid.

Gallup: A research-based, global performance-management-consulting company based in the United States that measures employee engagement in companies.

grand master: The highest title that a chess player can receive from the World Chess Federation.

head fake: A situation in which a player moves his or her head to fake a change in direction.

Herrmann Brain Dominance Instrument: A trademarked, survey-based assessment for thinking preferences based on a metaphoric model of the human brain developed by Ned Herrmann.

income statement: A financial report that tracks the revenue, expenses, and profit of a company; also called a P&L (profit and loss) statement.

information age: The age of the computer, in which people and organizations use machines to store, manipulate, and transmit data and information.

JIT (just in time): A management approach used to first reduce inventory to help optimize a manufacturing system and then use the optimized system to reduce ongoing inventory levels.

knowledge age: The era during which knowledge is the most important factor of production, and knowledge-work-productivity improvement is the most important focus of management.

knowledge work: Work that uses ideas, expertise, information, and relationships to achieve tasks; it includes brainstorming, analysis, project management, and personal coaching.

knowledge workers: Those who earn a living through knowledge work, including researchers, analysts, managers, consultants, and others.

knowledge-work productivity: The effectiveness and efficiency of knowledge workers to create, improve, and/or discontinue products, services, activities, and processes.

leadership: The ability to move people to a higher vision and a higher level of performance, grounded in strong management practices and high integrity.

management by objectives: A management approach originated by Peter F. Drucker in which specific objectives and measures focus on the efforts of individuals and the overall company.

management: The practice of organizing people to achieve better results as a group than they could attain as individuals to help customers lower their costs and be more successful.

market value: The value of a company's shares: similar to owning $100,000 equity in a $200,000 house. The combination of equity *and* debt of a company, or house, is the company's total (enterprise) value.

mental model: A framework that people have in their minds to interpret the world, such as "don't touch fire because it hurts." The model is invisible by nature but determines many behaviors.

Myers-Briggs Type Indicator: A psychometric survey to assess how people perceive the world; it uses psychological types developed by the Swiss psychiatrist Carl Jung.

operating profit: The money that a company earns after paying all its day-to-day expenses but before paying its taxes and interest payments on loans.

organizational logic: The logic embedded in an organization through its hierarchy, product-service menu, decision making, incentive designs, and centralization-decentralization lines.

paradigm: A school of thought that uses a single lens to view a collection of theories.

Parkinson's law: Cyril Northcote Parkinson's notion that work expands to fill the available time and that there is a natural tendency for staff members to accumulate.

Peter principle: Laurence J. Peter and Raymond Hull's principle that people rise to their level of incompetence in organizational hierarchies.

planned abandonment: Created by Peter Drucker, this idea highlights that planned, purposeful abandonment of the old and the unrewarding is a prerequisite to successful pursuit of the new and highly promising.

Playing to Win: A groundbreaking book and strategy process written and developed by A. G. Lafley and Roger L. Martin. The approach transcends the traditional scientific-management method used by most consulting firms. It is collaborative in nature and is very productive from a knowledge-work perspective.

PMLC: Abbreviation for the project-management life cycle.

productivity paradox: The observation—some even consider it a theory—that massive investments in IT have not resulted in productivity increases.

productivity: The combination of effectiveness and efficiency; it measures output divided by input in the short term and prosperity over the long run.

product-service menu: An approach for integrating products and services, with necessary capabilities to support them and clear communications to describe them.

project-management life cycle (PMLC): Integrated project-management approach linked to the EDBA process.

property rights: The right of individuals or groups to legally own something, and to do with it whatever they choose, while also excluding others from owning it.

return on assets: The size of your profits relative to the assets that it takes to generate them. A $1,000 profit on a $10,000 piece of equipment generates a 10 percent return on assets.

scientific management: Objective management techniques developed by Frederick Taylor, and a book by the same title, to improve manual-work productivity in the twentieth century.

sea change: A profound or notable transformation.

SG&A percentage: The selling, general, and administrative-expense percentage, which measures the percentage of day-to-day operating expenses required to generate the company's revenue.

shareholders: Individuals and firms owning a company. Their shares make up the company's market value, which is influenced by the profitability and growth of the firm.

silo: A silo is a tower or pit on a farm used to store grain. The term is also used to describe departments that work independently from one another and the rest of the company.

skin in the game: An expression for when someone is committed to something to the degree that he or she has something to lose if it is not successful.

social sciences: The study of people, as individuals and groups; it includes academic branches of study such as economics, sociology, psychology, and political science.

socio-systematic: The combination of a social science–based approach with an integrated implementation process, based on the work of Drucker, Burrell, Morgan, Wiener, Parsons, and Schwandt.

SP: Abbreviation for Strategic Profiling.

SP-AP: Abbreviation for Strategic Profiling–Action Planning.

Strategic Profiling (SP): A survey to understand the preferences, abilities, and priorities of knowledge workers in order to create better and faster solutions. It operationalizes the EDBA framework.

Strategic Profiling–Action Planning (SP-AP): The combination of the use of strategic profiling and facilitated sessions to cocreate cross-functional solutions and action plans.

supply chain: The movement of goods from suppliers to customers; it includes procurement, manufacturing, warehousing, and distribution functions.

system: A whole structure—whether mechanical, natural, or social—with interdependent parts. As such, the improvement of a single part will not improve the whole if the single part is not a constraint.

system dynamics: An important modeling technique created by Jay Forrester and popularized by Peter Senge that emphasizes the important effect of time delays and feedback loops on systems.

transformation-management office (TMO): The TMO described in this book is socio-systematic and integrates key velocity-advantage methods into traditional project-management routines.

velocity: Velocity is referred to in this book as the speed and direction of knowledge-based work; it is also described as knowledge-work productivity.

Acknowledgments

Management thinkers stand on the shoulders of many people; Peter Drucker was the tallest giant among them. As I write this, I am sitting in his office chair in his Claremont, California, home, now owned by the Drucker Institute. To my right are his handwritten notes on making knowledge productive. To my left is his Brother GX-6750 electronic typewriter, which he used to write the last ten of his thirty-nine books.

This book would not have been possible without a great deal of help. I owe a lot to the Drucker Institute team, a wonderful group of mentors and friends. Brand Velocity and Consequent employees and clients have also been instrumental. Alan Kisling, Dino Robusto, Oscar Munoz, Steve Voorhees, Fredrik Eliasson, Tom Miller, Bob Guido, and Shaun Higgins are certainly at the top of the list.

I am also indebted to many scholars. They include Drucker himself, who did more than anyone to foresee the need for the velocity advantage; Roger Martin, the prolific writer, teacher, and speaker; Peter Senge, who put systems thinking on the map; Thomas Davenport, who beautifully articulated many insights on knowledge work; and David Schwandt, who taught me how the social sciences can help people improve personal engagement and organizational performance.

Finally, I would like to thank Raman Bhardwaj for creating this book's illustrations and Dr. Merrill Ashcraft and Dorothy Vollmer for their support in editing this book.

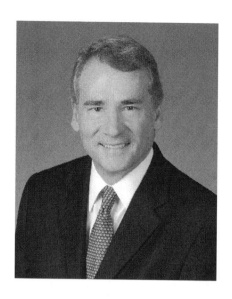

About the Author

Jack Bergstrand is the CEO and founder of Brand Velocity Inc. (BV) and Consequent Consulting. He is on the board of the Drucker Institute and is a leading expert on successfully managing large cross-functional initiatives. He specializes in business strategy and large business-transformation efforts. Prior to starting BV and Consequent, he was CIO of the Coca-Cola Company, CFO and head of manufacturing and logistics for Coca-Cola Beverages, and chief marketing officer and division manager for the Coca-Cola Bottling Company of New England. Jack has three master's degrees: in management from the Stanford Graduate School of Business, in education and human development from George Washington University, and in advertising from Michigan State University.

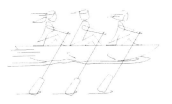

Bibliography

Aaker, David A. *Building Strong Brands*. New York: Free Press, 1996.

Aaker, David A., and Damien McLoughlin. *Strategic Market Management*. Hoboken, NJ: Wiley, 2007.

Abidi, Suhayl, and Manoj Joshi. *The VUCA Company*. Mumbai, India: Jaico Publishing House, 2015.

Ackermann, Fran, Colin Eden, and Steve Cropper. "Getting Started with Cognitive Mapping." Proceedings of the 7th Young Operational Research Conference. University of Warwick, Coventry, UK, 1992.

Adair-Heeley, Charlene B. *The Human Side of Just-in-Time: How to Make the Techniques Really Work*. New York: American Management Association, 1991.

Allison, Graham T., and Philip Zelikow. *Essence of Decision: Explaining the Cuban Missile Crisis*. 2nd ed. New York: Longman, 1999.

Andreas, Steve, and Charles Faulkner, eds. *NLP: The New Technology of Achievement*. New York: Quill, 1994.

The Arbinger Institute. *Leadership and Self-Deception: Getting Out of the Box*. San Francisco: Berrett-Koehler, 2000.

Ash, Mary Kay. *Mary Kay on People Management*. New York: Warner Books, 1984.

———. *Miracles Happen: The Life and Timeless Principles of the Founder of Mary Kay Inc.* New York: HarperCollins, 2003.

Bach, George L., and Robert J. Flanagan. *Macroeconomics: Analysis, Decision Making, and Policy.* 11th ed. Englewood Cliffs, NJ: Prentice Hall, 1987.

Baghai, Mehrdad, Stephen Coley, and David White. *The Alchemy of Growth: Practical Insights for Building the Enduring Enterprise.* Reading, MA: Perseus Books, 1999.

Ballou, Ronald H. *Business Logistics Management: Planning, Organizing, and Controlling the Supply Chain.* 4th ed. Upper Saddle River, NJ: Prentice Hall, 1999.

Barnard, Chester I. *The Functions of the Executive.* Cambridge, MA: Harvard University Press, 1968.

Bartlett, Joseph W. *Fundamentals of Venture Capital.* Lanham, MD: Madison Books, 1999.

Beckhard, Richard, and Wendy Pritchard. *Changing the Essence: The Art of Creating and Leading Fundamental Change in Organizations.* San Francisco: Jossey-Bass, 1992.

Bell, Daniel. *The Coming of Post-Industrial Society: A Venture in Social Forecasting.* New York: Basic Books, 1973.

Bennis, Warren G., and Burt Nanus. *Leaders: Strategies for Taking Charge.* 2nd ed. New York: Harper Business, 1997.

Bennis, Warren G., Gretchen M. Spreitzer, and Thomas G. Cummings. *The Future of Leadership: Today's Top Leadership Thinkers Speak to Tomorrow's Leaders.* San Francisco: Jossey-Bass, 2001.

Bergstrand, Jack. *Reinvent Your Enterprise: Through Better Knowledge Work.* Charleston, SC: Book Surge Publishing, 2009.

———. *The Velocity Advantage.* 1st ed. Atlanta, GA: Brand Velocity, 2016.

Blanchard, Benjamin S. *Logistics Engineering and Management.* 6th ed. Upper Saddle River, NJ: Pearson Prentice Hall, 2004.

Blanchard, Ken H. *The Heart of a Leader*. Tulsa, OK: Honor Books, 1999.

Blanchard, Ken H., and Spencer Johnson. *The One Minute Manager*. 10th ed. New York: Berkley Books, 1983.

Bluth, B. J. *Parsons' General Theory of Action: A Summary of the Basic Theory*. Granada Hills, CA: NBS, 1982.

Bly, Robert W. *Keeping Clients Satisfied: Make Your Service Business More Successful and Profitable*. Englewood Cliffs, NJ: Prentice Hall, 1993.

Bonoma, Thomas V. *The Marketing Edge: Making Strategies Work*. New York: Free Press, 1985.

Bowersox, Donald J. *Leading Edge Logistics: Competitive Positioning for the 1990s: Comprehensive Research on Logistics Organization, Strategy and Behavior in North America*. Oak Brook, IL: Council of Logistics Management, 1989.

Buchanan, Leigh. "10 Traits of a Drucker-Like Leader." *Inc.*, December 13, 2013.

Buford, Bob. *Game Plan: Winning Strategies for the Second Half of Your Life*. Grand Rapids, MI: Zondervan, 1998.

———. *Halftime: Changing Your Game Plan from Success to Significance*. Grand Rapids, MI: Zondervan, 1994.

Burrell, Gibson, and Gareth Morgan. *Sociological Paradigms and Organisational Analysis: Elements of the Sociology of Corporate Life*. London: Heinemann. 1979.

Byrne, John A. "The Man Who Invented Management: Why Peter Drucker's Ideas Still Matter." *BusinessWeek*, November 28, 2005.

Carnegie, Dale. *How to Win Friends and Influence People*. New York: Pocket Books, 1982.

Castaneda, Carlos. *A Separate Reality: Further Conversations with Don Juan*. New York: Simon & Schuster, 1971.

Chapman, Alan. "Conscious Competence Learning Model." *Businessballs.com*, 2007.

————. "Pareto's Principle: The 80-20 Rule, Pareto's Law, or Pareto Theory." *Businessballs.com*, n.d.

Chopra, Deepak. *The Seven Spiritual Laws of Success: A Pocketbook Guide to Fulfilling Your Dreams.* San Rafael, CA: Harmony, 2007.

————. *The Way of the Wizard: Twenty Spiritual Lessons in Creating the Life You Want.* New York: Harmony Books, 1995.

Christensen, Clayton M., and Michael E. Raynor. *The Innovator's Solution: Creating and Sustaining Successful Growth.* Boston: Harvard Business School Press, 2003.

Coase, Ronald Harry. *Essays on Economics and Economists.* Chicago: University of Chicago Press, 1994.

————. *The Nature of the Firm: Origins, Evolution, and Development.* Edited by Oliver E. Williamson and Sidney G. Winter. New York: Oxford University Press. 1991.

Coffield, Frank, David Moseley, Elaine Hall, and Kathryn Ecclestone. *Learning Styles and Pedagogy in Post-16 Learning: A Systematic and Critical Review.* London: Learning and Skills Research Centre, 2004.

Collins, James Charles, and Jerry I. Porras. *Built to Last: Successful Habits of Visionary Companies.* New York: Harper Business, 1994.

Cook, Melissa A. *Building Enterprise Information Architectures: Reengineering Information Systems.* Upper Saddle River, NJ: Prentice Hall, 1996.

Copeland, Tom E., Tim Koller, and Jack Murrin. *Valuation: Measuring and Managing the Value of Companies.* 3rd ed. New York: Wiley, 2000.

Cortada, James W. *Best Practices in Information Technology: How Corporations Get the Most Value from Exploiting Their Digital Investments.* Upper Saddle River, NJ: Prentice Hall, 1998.

Covey, Stephen R. *The 7 Habits of Highly Effective People: Powerful Lessons in Personal Change*. New York: Free Press, 2004.

Coyle, John Joseph, Edward J. Bardi, and C. John Langley. *The Management of Business Logistics*. 6th ed. Minneapolis, MN: West Publishing Co., 1996.

Crum, Thomas F. *Journey to Center: Lessons in Unifying Body, Mind, and Spirit*. New York: Simon & Schuster, 1997.

Cusumano, Michael A., and Richard W. Selby. *Microsoft Secrets: How the World's Most Powerful Software Company Creates Technology, Shapes Markets, and Manages People*. New York: Free Press, 1995.

Damodaran, Aswath. *Damodaran on Valuation: Security Analysis for Investment and Corporate Finance*. 2nd ed. Hoboken, NJ: John Wiley & Sons, 2006.

Davenport, Thomas H. *Process Innovation: Reengineering Work through Information Technology*. Boston: Harvard Business School Press, 1993.

———. *Thinking for a Living: How to Get Better Performance and Results from Knowledge Workers*. Boston: Harvard Business School Press, 2005.

———. "Was Drucker Wrong?" Babsonknowledge.org, December 26, 2005.

Davenport, Thomas H., and Laurence Prusak. *Information Ecology: Mastering the Information and Knowledge Environment*. New York: Oxford University Press, 1997.

Davis, Stanley M., and Christopher Meyer. *Blur: The Speed of Change in the Connected Economy*. Reading, MA: Addison-Wesley, 1998.

Davis, Stanley M., and William H. Davidson. *2020 Vision*. New York: Simon & Schuster, 1991.

De Pree, Max. *Leadership Jazz*. New York: Dell Publishing, 1992.

Denver, John, and Mike Taylor. "Rocky Mountain High." *Rocky Mountain High*. RCA, 1972.

Dewey, John. *Democracy and Education*. New York: Barnes & Noble Books, 2005.

Dosher, Marion, Otis Benepe, Albert Humphrey, Robert Stewart, and Birger Lie. *The SWOT Analysis Method*. Menlo Park, CA: Stanford Research Institute, 1960.

Drucker, Peter F. *The Age of Discontinuity: Guidelines to Our Changing Society*. New York: Harper & Row, 1969.

———. *The Effective Executive*. London: Heinemann, 1967.

———. "The Future Has Already Happened." *The Futurist* 32, no. 8 (1998).

———. *Innovation and Entrepreneurship: Practice and Principles*. New York: Harper & Row, 1985.

———. "Knowledge Work." *Executive Excellence* 19, no. 10 (2002).

———. "Knowledge-Worker Productivity: The Biggest Challenge." *California Management Review* 41, no. 2 (1999).

———. *Management Challenges for the 21st Century*. New York: Harper Business, 1999.

———. *Management: Tasks, Responsibilities, Practices*. New Brunswick, NJ: Transaction Publishers, 2007.

———. *Managing for Results: Economic Tasks and Risk-Taking Decisions*. New York: Perennial Library, 1986.

———. *Managing in the Next Society*. New York: Saint Martin's Press, 1994.

———. "The New Meaning of Corporate Social Responsibility." *California Management Review* 26, no. 2 (1984).

———. *The Pension Fund Revolution*. New Brunswick, NJ: Transaction Publishers, 1996.

———. *Peter Drucker on the Profession of Management*. Boston: Harvard Business School Press, 1998.

———. *Post-Capitalist Society*. New York: Harper Business, 1993.

————. *The Practice of Management.* New York: Perennial Library. 1986.

Duncan, Tom, and Sandra E. Moriarty. *Driving Brand Value: Using Integrated Marketing to Manage Profitable Stakeholder Relationships.* New York: McGraw-Hill, 1997.

Dutton, Jane E., and Janet M. Dukerich. "Keeping an Eye on the Mirror: Image and Identity in Organizational Adaptation." *The Academy of Management Journal* (1991).

Einstein, Albert, and Carl Seelig. *Ideas and Opinions.* 3rd ed. New York: Crown Trade Paperbacks, 1995.

Eisenhardt, Kathleen M. "Agency Theory: An Assessment and Review." *Academy of Management Review* 14, no. 1 (1989): 57–74.

Evans, Dylan. *Emotion: The Science of Sentiment.* Oxford, UK: Oxford University Press, 2001.

Fairley, Stephen G., and Chris E. Stout. *Getting Started in Personal and Executive Coaching: How to Create a Thriving Coaching Practice.* Hoboken, NJ: John Wiley & Sons, 2004.

Fiol, C. Marlene, and Marjorie A. Lyles. "Organizational Learning." *Academy of Management Review* 10, no. 4 (1985): 803–13.

Fiske, Susan T., and Shelley E. Taylor. *Social Cognition: From Brains to Culture.* Boston: McGraw-Hill Higher Education, 2008.

Forbes Inc. *Forbes Richest People: The Forbes Annual Profile of the World's Wealthiest Men and Women.* New York: John Wiley & Sons: 2007.

Ford, Nigel, and Sherry Y. Chen. "Matching/Mismatching Revisited: An Empirical Study of Learning and Teaching Styles." *British Journal of Educational Technology* 32, no. 1 (2001): 5–22.

Forrester, Jay W. *Principes des systèmes*. Translated by Patrick Sylvestre-Baron. 3rd ed. Lyon, France: Presses Universitaires de Lyon, 1984.

Frankl, Viktor E. *Man's Search for Meaning*. Boston: Beacon Press, 2006.

Garland, Diana, and Barbara N. Martin. "Do Gender and Learning Style Play a Role in How Online Courses Should Be Designed?" *Journal of Interactive Online Learning* 4, no. 2 (2005): 4–9.

Gates, Bill, and Collins Hemingway. *Business @ the Speed of Thought: Using a Digital Nervous System*, 470. New York: Warner Books, 1999.

Gates, Bill, Nathan Myhrvold, and Peter Rinearson. *The Road Ahead*, 332. New York: Penguin Books, 1996.

Geneen, Harold, and Alvin Moscow. *Managing*. Garden City, NY: Doubleday, 1984.

Gerber, Michael E. *The E-Myth: Why Most Businesses Don't Work and What to Do about It*. Cambridge, MA: Ballinger Publishing, 1986.

———. *The E-Myth Revisited: Why Most Small Businesses Don't Work and What to Do about It*. New York: Harper Business, 1995.

Getty, J. Paul. *How to Be Rich*. New York: Jove Book, 1983.

Gladstone, David, and Laura Gladstone. *Venture Capital Handbook: An Entrepreneur's Guide to Raising Venture Capital*. Upper Saddle River, NJ: Prentice Hall, 2002.

Gobet, Fernand, Peter C. R. Lane, Steve Croker, Peter C-H. Cheng, Gary Jones, Iain Oliver, and Julian M. Pine. "Chunking Mechanisms in Human Learning." *Trends in Cognitive Science* 5.6 (2001): 236–43.

Goldratt, Eliyahu M. *The Goal: A Process of Ongoing Improvement*. 3rd ed. Burlington, VT: Gower, 2004.

———. *What Is This Thing Called Theory of Constraints and How*

Should It Be Implemented? Croton-on-Hudson, NY: North River Press, 1990.

Goldratt, Eliyahu M., and Jeff Cox. *The Goal: Excellence in Manufacturing.* Croton-on-Hudson, NY: North River Press, 1984.

Goldston, Mark R. *The Turnaround Prescription: Repositioning Troubled Companies.* New York: Free Press, 1992.

Goleman, Daniel P. *Emotional Intelligence.* New York: Bantam Books, 2006.

———. *Harvard Business Review* on *What Makes a Leader.* Boston: Harvard Business School Publishing Corporation, 2001.

Gordon, Ian. *Relationship Marketing: New Strategies, Techniques, and Technologies to Win the Customers You Want and Keep Them Forever.* New York: John Wiley & Sons, 1998.

Grobman, Gary M. "Complexity Theory: A New Way to Look at Organizational Change." *Public Administration Quarterly* (2005).

Hagstrom, Robert G. *The Warren Buffett Way: Investment Strategies of the World's Greatest Investor.* New York: John Wiley, 1995.

Halbwachs, Maurice, and Lewis A. Closer. *On Collective Memory.* Chicago: University of Chicago Press, 1992.

Hall, Robert E., and John B. Taylor. *Macroeconomics.* 5th ed. New York: W. W. Norton & Co., 1997.

Haller, Terry. *Secrets of the Master Business Strategists.* Englewood Cliffs, NJ: Prentice Hall, 1983.

Hamel, Gary, and Coimbatore K. Prahalad. "Strategic Intent." *Harvard Business Review* (1989).

Hammer, Michael, and James Champy. *Reengineering the Corporation: A Manifesto for Business Revolution.* New York: Harper Business Essentials, 2003.

Hardy-Vallee, Benoit. "The Cost of Bad Project Management." *Gallup*, February 7, 2012.

Harrell, Wilson. *For Entrepreneurs Only*. Franklin Lakes, NJ: Career Press, 1995.

Harvard Business Review. *The New Manufacturing*. Boston, MA: Harvard Business School Press, 1991.

Harvard Business School. *Harvard Business Essentials: Strategy: Create and Implement the Best Strategy for Your Business*. Boston: Harvard Business School Press, 2005.

Hayes, Robert H., Steven C. Wheelwright, and Kim B. Clark. *Dynamic Manufacturing: Creating the Learning Organization*. New York: Simon & Schuster, 1988.

Henderson, Bruce. *The Product Portfolio*. BCG Perspective Series. Boston: The Boston Consulting Group, 1970.

Herrmann, Ned. *The Creative Brain*. Lake Lure, NC: Brain Books, 1988.

———. *The Whole Brain Business Book*. New York: McGraw-Hill, 1996.

Hill, Napoleon. *The Law of Success*. Northbrook, IL: Napoleon Hill Foundation, 1997.

———. *Think and Grow Rich*. Mineola, NY: Dover Publications, 2007.

Hlupic, Vlatka. "Hack: Using 'Traditionally Virtual' Organizational Structure." *Management Innovation eXchange*, April 26, 2012.

———. "Hack: Why Points Trump the Hierarchy to Reward Contribution in Knowledge Organizations." *Management Innovation eXchange*, April 26, 2012.

———. *The Management Shift: How to Harness the Power of People and Transform Your Organization for Sustainable Success*. London: Palgrave Macmillan, 2014.

Holmes, Oliver Wendell. *"The One-Hoss Shay," "The Chambered Nautilus," and Other Poems, Gay and Grave*. Boston: Houghton, Mifflin and Company, 1900.

Hutchinson, Sarah E., and Stacey C. Sawyer. *Computers and Information Systems*. Burr Ridge, IL: Richard D. Irwin Inc., 1994.

Ichijo, Kazuo, and Ikujiro Nonaka, eds. *Knowledge Creation and Management: New Challenges for Managers.* New York: Oxford University Press, 2006.

James, Barrie G. *Business Wargames.* Cambridge, MA: Abacus Press, 1985.

Janssen, Jeff. *Championship Team Building: What Every Coach Needs to Know to Build a Motivated, Committed & Cohesive Team.* Tucson, AZ: Janssen Peak Performance Inc., 2002.

Jaques, Elliott, and Kathryn Cason. *Human Capability: A Study of Individual Potential and Its Application.* Falls Church, VA: Cason Hall & Co., 1994.

Jones, Laurie B. *Jesus, CEO: Using Ancient Wisdom for Visionary Leadership.* New York: Hyperion, 1995.

Jung, Carl G. *Psychological Types.* Princeton, NJ: Princeton University Press, 1976.

———. *Four Archetypes: Mother, Rebirth, Spirit, Trickster.* Translated by R. F. C. Hull. London: Routledge and Paul Kegan PLC, 1972.

Kalakota, Ravi, and Marcia Robinson. *E-Business: Roadmap for Success.* Reading, MA: Addison-Wesley, 1999.

Kanter, Rosabeth M. *When Giants Learn to Dance.* New York: Simon & Schuster, 1989.

Katz, Daniel, and Robert L. Kahn. *The Social Psychology of Organizations.* 2nd ed. New York: Wiley, 1978.

Kawasaki, Guy. *The Art of the Start: The Time-Tested, Battle-Hardened Guide for Anyone Starting Anything.* New York: Portfolio, 2004.

Keirsey, David. *Please Understand Me II: Temperament, Character, Intelligence.* Del Mar, CA: Prometheus Nemesis, 1998.

Keller, Kevin L. *Strategic Brand Management: Building, Measuring, and Managing Brand Equity.* 3rd ed. Upper Saddle River, NJ: Prentice Hall, 2008.

Kelly, Kevin. *Out of Control: The Rise of Neo-Biological Civilization*. Reading, MA: Addison-Wesley, 1994.

Kempis, Rolf-Dieter, and Jürgen Ringbeck. *Do IT Smart: Seven Rules for Superior Information Technology Performance*. New York: Free Press, 1999.

Keup, Erwin J. *Franchise Bible: How to Buy a Franchise or Franchise Your Own Business*. 6th ed. Irvine, CA: Entrepreneur Press, 2007.

Kochan, Nick. *The World's Greatest Brands*. New York: New York University Press, 1997.

Kolb, David A. *Experiential Learning: Experience as the Source of Learning and Development*. Englewood Cliffs, NJ: Prentice Hall, 1984.

Kotler, Philip, and Kevin L. Keller. *Marketing Management*. 12th ed. Upper Saddle River, NJ: Pearson Prentice Hall, 2006.

Kotter, John P. *Leading Change*. Boston: Harvard Business School Press, 2012.

Krajewski, Lee J., and Larry P. Ritzman. *Operations Management: Strategy and Analysis*. 6th ed. Upper Saddle River, NJ: Prentice Hall, 2002.

Krames, Jeffrey A. *Inside Drucker's Brain*. New York: Portfolio, 2008.

Kroc, Ray, and Robert Anderson. *Grinding It Out: The Making of McDonald's*. Chicago: Henry Regnery Company, 1977.

Kuhn, Thomas S. *The Structure of Scientific Revolutions*. 3rd ed. Chicago: University of Chicago Press, 1996.

Lafley, Alan G., and Roger L. Martin. *Playing to Win: How Strategy Really Works*. Boston: Harvard Business Press, 2013.

Lao-Tzu. *Tao Te Ching: A New English Version*. Translated by Stephen Mitchell. New York: HarperCollins, 1988.

Lawrence, Gordon D. *Looking at Type and Learning Styles*. Gainesville, FL: Center for Applications of Psychological Type Inc., 1997.

Levine, Rick, Christopher Locke, Doc Searls, and David Weinberger. *The Cluetrain Manifesto: The End of Business as Usual.* Cambridge, MA: Perseus Books, 2000.

Levinthal, Daniel A., and James G. March. "The Myopia of Learning." *Strategic Management Journal* (1993).

Levitt, Barbara, and James G. March. "Organizational Learning." *Annual Review of Sociology* 14 (1988).

Lewis, Michael. *The New Thing: A Silicon Valley Story.* New York: W. W. Norton, 2000.

Lipnack, Jessica, and Jeffrey Stamps. *The Age of the Network: Organizing Principles for the 21st Century.* New York: Wiley. 1994.

Lopker, John. *Pictures of Personality: Guide to the Four Human Natures.* Los Angeles: Typology, 2000.

Lowe, Janet. *Bill Gates Speaks: Insight from the World's Greatest Entrepreneur.* New York: John Wiley, 1998.

———. *Warren Buffett Speaks: Wit and Wisdom from the World's Greatest Investor.* Hoboken, NJ: John Wiley & Sons, 2007.

Madnick, Stuart E. *The Strategic Use of Information Technology.* New York: Oxford University Press, 1987.

Magee, John F., William C. Copacino, and Donald B. Rosenfield. *Modern Logistics Management: Integrating Marketing, Manufacturing, and Physical Distribution.* New York: John Wiley, 1985.

Marquardt, Michael J. *Action Learning in Action: Transforming Problems and People for World-Class Organizational Learning.* Palo Alto, CA: Davies-Black Publications, 1999.

———. *Leading with Questions: How Leaders Find the Right Solutions by Knowing What to Ask.* San Francisco: Jossey-Bass, 2005.

Marren, Joseph H. *Mergers & Acquisitions: A Valuation Handbook.* Homewood, IL: Business One Irwin, 1993.

Martin, Don. *Team Think: Using the Sports Connection to Develop, Motivate, and Manage a Winning Business.* New York: Plume, 1994.

Martin, Roger L. "Rethinking the Decision Factory." *Harvard Business Review* 91 (2013).

McGregor, John D. "Complexity, It's in the Mind of the Beholder." *Journal of Object Technology* 5, no. 1 (2006).

McNally, David, and Karl D. Speak. *Be Your Own Brand: A Breakthrough Formula for Standing out from the Crowd.* San Francisco: Berrett-Koehler, 2002.

Merriam, Sharan B., Rosemary S. Caffarella, and Lisa M. Baumgartner. *Learning in Adulthood: A Comprehensive Guide.* 3rd ed. San Francisco: Jossey-Bass, 2007.

Metcalfe, Robert M. "It's All in Your Head: The Latest Supercomputer Is Way Faster than the Human Brain. But Guess Which Is Smarter?" *Forbes* 179 (2007).

Mezirow, Jack. "Understanding Transformation Theory." *Adult Education Quarterly* 44 (1994).

Miller, James B., and Paul B. Brown. *The Corporate Coach.* New York: Harper Business, 1994.

Murphy, Emmett C., and Michael Snell. *The Genius of Sitting Bull.* Englewood Cliffs, NJ: Prentice Hall, 1993.

Myers, Isabel B., and M. H. McCaulley. *A Guide to the Development and Use of the Myers-Briggs Type Indicator.* 3rd ed. Palo Alto, CA: Consulting Psychologists Press, 1998.

Myers, Isabel B., and Peter B. Myers. *Gifts Differing.* 10th ed. Palo Alto, CA: Consulting Psychologists Press, 1990.

———. *Gifts Differing: Understanding Personality Type.* Palo Alto, CA: Davies-Black Publishers, 1995.

Nadler, David, Marc S. Gerstein, and Robert B. Shaw. *Organizational Architecture: Designs for Changing Organizations.* San Francisco: Jossey-Bass, 1992.

Nelson, Roy Paul. *The Design of Advertising.* 7th ed. Madison, WI: Brown & Benchmark, 1994.

Norman, Donald A. *The Design of Everyday Things.* New York: Basic Books, 2002.

North, Douglas Cecil. *Structure and Change in Economic History.* New York: Norton, 1981.

O'Gorman, James F. *ABC of Architecture.* Philadelphia: University of Pennsylvania Press, 1998.

Ohmae, Kenichi I. *The Mind of the Strategist.* New York: Penguin Books, 1983.

Oster, Sharon M. *Modern Competitive Analysis.* 3rd ed. New York: Oxford University Press, 1999.

Parkinson, Cyril N. *Parkinson's Law and Other Studies in Administration.* Boston: Houghton Mifflin, 1957.

Parsi, Novid. "2015 Global Job Report." *Project Management Network,* January 2015.

Parsons, Talcott. *Action Theory and the Human Condition.* New York: Free Press, 1978.

———. *The Structure of Social Action.* New York: McGraw-Hill, 1937.

Parsons, Talcott, and Edward Shils. *Toward a General Theory of Action.* Cambridge, MA: Harvard University Press, 1951.

Parsons, Talcott, R. F. Bales, and Edward Shils. *Working Papers in the Theory of Action.* Glencoe, IL: Free Press, 1953.

Patterson, Marvin L., and Sam Lightman. *Accelerating Innovation: Improving the Process of Product Development.* New York: Van Nostrand Reinhold, 1993.

Peppers, Don, and Martha Rogers. *The One-to-One Manager: Real-World Lessons in Customer Relationship Management.* New York: Doubleday, 1999.

Perry, Lee T., W. Norman Smallwood, and Randell G. Stott. *Real-Time Strategy: Improvising Team-Based Planning for a Fast-Changing World.* New York: Wiley, 1993.

Peter, Laurence J. *Why Things Go Wrong, or The Peter Principle Revisited.* New York: McGraw-Hill, 1985.

Peters, Thomas J., and Robert H. Waterman. *In Search of Excellence: Lessons from America's Best-Run Companies.* New York: Harper Business Essentials, 2004.

Pfeffer, Jeffrey. *Competitive Advantage through People: Unleashing the Power of the Work Force.* Boston: Harvard Business School Press, 1994.

Pfeffer, Jeffrey, and Robert I. Sutton. *The Knowing-Doing Gap: How Smart Companies Turn Knowledge into Action.* Boston: Harvard Business School Press, 2000.

Piderit, Sandy K. "Rethinking Resistance and Recognizing Ambivalence: A Multidimensional View of Attitudes toward an Organizational Change." *Academy of Management Review* 25 (2000).

Pirsig, Robert M. *Zen and the Art of Motorcycle Maintenance: An Inquiry into Values.* Quill ed. New York: W. Morrow, 1999.

Pollan, Stephen M., and Mark Levine. *The Field Guide to Starting a Business.* New York: Simon & Schuster, 1990.

Porch, Germaine, and Jed Niederer. *Coach Anyone about Anything: How to Help People Succeed in Business and Life.* Del Mar, CA: Wharton Publishing Inc.

Porras, Jerry I. *Stream Analysis: A Powerful Way to Diagnose and Manage Organizational Change.* Reading, MA: Addison-Wesley, 1987.

Porter, Michael E. *Competitive Advantage: Creating and Sustaining Superior Performance: With a New Introduction.* New York: Free Press, 1998.

———. *The Competitive Advantage of Nations: With a New Introduction.* New York: Free Press, 1998.

———. *Competitive Strategy: Techniques for Analyzing Industries and Competitors: With a New Introduction.* New York: Free Press, 1998.

————. *Michael E. Porter on Competition and Strategy.* Cambridge, MA: Harvard Business School, 1991.

Project Management Institute. *A Guide to the Project Management Body of Knowledge.* 3rd ed. Newtown Square, PA: Project Management Institute Inc., 2004.

Puri, Subhash C. *ISO 9000 Certification: Total Quality Management.* Ottawa, Canada: Standards Quality Management Group, 1992.

Quindlen, Ruthann. *Confessions of a Venture Capitalist: Inside the High-Stakes World of Start-Up Financing.* New York: Warner Books, 2002.

Rescher, Nicholas. *Process Metaphysics: An Introduction to Process Philosophy.* Albany: State University of New York Press, 1996.

Ries, Al, and Laura Ries. *The 22 Immutable Laws of Branding: How to Build a Product or Service into a World-Class Brand.* New York: Harper Business, 2002.

Ries, Al, and Jack Trout. *Positioning: The Battle for Your Mind.* New York: McGraw-Hill, 2001.

Rouse, William B. *Enterprise Transformation: Understanding and Enabling Fundamental Change.* Hoboken, NJ: Wiley-Interscience, 2006.

Saloner, Garth, Andrea Shepard, and Joel M. Podolny. *Strategic Management.* New York: John Wiley, 2001.

Sashkin, Marshall, and Molly G. Sashkin. *Leadership That Matters: The Critical Factors for Making a Difference in People's Lives and Organizations' Success.* San Francisco: Berrett-Koehler, 2003.

Schön, Donald A. *Educating the Reflective Practitioner: Toward a New Design for Teaching and Learning in the Professions.* San Francisco: Jossey-Bass, 1987.

Schonberger, R. *World-Class Manufacturing: The Lessons of Simplicity Applied.* New York: Free Press, 1986.

Schuller, Robert H. *Discover Your Possibilities*. New York: Ballantine Books, 1986.

———. *Your Church Has a Fantastic Future! A Possibility Thinker's Guide to a Successful Church*. Ventura, CA: Regal Books, 1986.

Schwandt, David R., and Michael J. Marquardt. *Organizational Learning: From World-Class Theories to Global Best Practices*. Boca Raton, FL: Saint Lucie Press, 2005.

Segil, Larraine. *Fastalliances: Power Your E-Business*. New York: John Wiley & Sons, 2001.

———. *Intelligent Business Alliances: How to Profit Using Today's Most Important Strategic Tool*. New York: Times Business, 1996.

Senge, Peter M. *The Fifth Discipline: The Art and Practice of the Learning Organization*. New York: Doubleday/Currency, 2006.

———. *The Fifth Discipline Fieldbook: Strategies and Tools for Building a Learning Organization*. New York: Currency, Doubleday, 1994.

Seybold, Patricia B., and Ronni T. Marshak. *Customers.com: How to Create a Profitable Business Strategy for the Internet and Beyond*. New York: Times Business, 1998.

Shapiro, Howard M. *Partnering: The New Way to Lead*. Osborne Park, WA: Persona Publishing, 2008.

Sherman, Andrew J. *Franchising & Licensing: Two Powerful Ways to Grow Your Business in Any Economy*. 3rd ed. New York: American Management Association, 2004.

Sieden, Lloyd Steven. *Buckminster Fuller's Universe*. Cambridge, MA: Basic Books. 2000.

Singer, Margaret T. *Cults in Our Midst*. San Francisco: Jossey-Bass, 2003.

Slywotzky, Adrian J., David Morrison, and Karl Weber. *How Digital Is Your Business?* New York: Crown Business, 2000.

Smith, Adam. *The Wealth of Nations*. New York: E. P. Dutton & Co., 1933.

Smith, Adam, and Edwin Cannan. *The Wealth of Nations*. New York: Modern Library, 2000.

Smith, Douglas K., and Robert C. Alexander. *Fumbling the Future: How Xerox Invented, Then Ignored, the First Personal Computer*. New York: William Morrow and Company, 1988.

Spender, J. C. "Making Knowledge the Basis of a Dynamic Theory of the Firm." *Strategic Management Journal* 17 (1996).

Stahl, Jack. *Lessons on Leadership: The 7 Fundamental Management Skills for Leaders at All Levels*. New York: Kaplan Publishing, 2007.

The Standish Group Report. "The CHAOS Report (1994)." The Standish Group, 1994.

Stasey, Robert, and Carol J. McNair. *Crossroads: A JIT Success Story*. Homewood, IL: Dow Jones/Irwin, 1990.

Stewart, Thomas A. *Intellectual Capital: The New Wealth of Organizations*. New York: Currency Doubleday, 1997.

Stewart III, G. Bennet. *The Quest for Value: A Guide for Senior Managers*. New York: Harper Business, 1991.

Stock, James R., and Douglas M. Lambert. *Strategic Logistics Management*. 4th ed. Boston: McGraw-Hill/Irwin, 2001.

Swanson, James A., and Michael L. Baird. *Engineering Your Start-Up: A Guide for the High-Tech Entrepreneur*. 2nd ed. Belmont, CA: Professional Publications, 2003.

Tapscott, Don, Alex Lowy, and David Ticoll, eds. *Blueprint to the Digital Economy: Creating Wealth in the Era of E-Business*. New York: McGraw-Hill, 1998.

Taylor, Frederick W. *The Principles of Scientific Management*. Jackson Hole, WY: Archeion Press, 2007. Thurow, Lester C. *Building Wealth: The New Rules for Individuals,*

Companies, and Nations in a Knowledge-Based Economy. New York: Granite Hill Publishers, 1999.

Toffler, Alvin, ed. *Learning for Tomorrow: The Role of the Future in Education.* New York: Vintage Books, 1974.

———. "Revolutionary Wealth." *New Perspectives Quarterly* 30, no. 4 (2013).

———. *The Third Wave.* New York: Bantam Books, 1981.

Treacy, Michael, and Frederick D. Wiersema. *The Discipline of Market Leaders: Choose Your Customers, Narrow Your Focus, Dominate Your Market.* Reading, MA: Addison-Wesley, 1997.

Triplett, Jack E. "The Solow Productivity Paradox: What Do Computers Do to Productivity?" *The Canadian Journal of Economics / Revue canadienne d'economique* 32, no. 2 (1999).

Turchin, Valentin F. *The Phenomenon of Science.* New York: Columbia University Press, 1977.

US Bureau of Labor Statistics. "Industrial Employment and Output Projections to 2014." *Monthly Labor Review,* December 2015.

Van Fleet, James K. *Lifetime Conversation Guide.* Englewood Cliffs, NJ: Prentice Hall, 1984.

Van Horne, James C. *Financial Management and Policy.* 12th ed. Upper Saddle River, NJ: Prentice Hall, 2002.

Van Horne, James C., and John Martin Wachowicz. *Fundamentals of Financial Management.* 11th ed. Upper Saddle River, NJ: Prentice Hall, 2001.

"Wall Street Journal Forecasting Survey for 2007." *Wall Street Journal.* New York ed., February 2007.

Walton, Sam, and John Huey. *Sam Walton, Made in America: My Story.* New York: Doubleday, 1992.

Waterman, Robert H. *Adhocracy: The Power to Change.* Knoxville, TN: Whittle Direct Books, 1990.

Watson, Stephen R., and Dennis M. Buede. *Decision Synthesis: The Principles and Practice of Decision Analysis.* Cambridge, UK: Cambridge University Press, 1987.

Weick, Karl E. *The Social Psychology of Organizing.* 2nd ed. Reading, MA: Addison-Wesley, 1979.

Weiner, Richard. *Professional's Guide to Publicity.* New York: Public Relations Publishing Co., 1975.

Weisbord, Marvin R. *Productive Workplaces Revisited: Dignity, Meaning, and Community in the 21st Century.* 2nd ed. San Francisco: John Wiley & Sons, 2004.

Wheatley, Margaret J. *Leadership and the New Science: Learning about Organization from an Orderly Universe.* San Francisco: Berrett-Koehler, 1992.

Whitehead, Alfred N., David R. Griffin, and Donald W. Sherburne. *Process and Reality: An Essay in Cosmology.* New York: Free Press, 1978.

Wiener, Norbert. *The Human Use of Human Beings: Cybernetics and Society.* New York: Da Capo Press, 1988.

Wilson, Robert A. *Prometheus Rising.* Phoenix, AZ: Falcon Press, 1983.

Wiskup, Mark. *The "It" Factor: Be the One People Like, Listen to, and Remember.* New York: American Management Association, 2007.

Wright, Frank L. *Frank Lloyd Wright and the Living City.* Edited by David Gilson De Long. Weil am Rhein, Germany: Vitra Design Museum, 1998.

Yukl, Gary A. *Leadership in Organizations.* 6th ed. Upper Saddle River, NJ: Pearson Prentice Hall, 2006.

Zald, Mayer N. "More Fragmentation? Unfinished Business in Linking the Social Sciences and the Humanities." *Administrative Science Quarterly* 41 (1996).

Zhenhui, Rao. "Matching Teaching Styles with Learning Styles in East Asian Contexts." *The Internet TESL Journal* 7 (2001).

Index

and branding, 112–13
and change management, 104
and coaching, 101
cross-functional strategies
  improved via, 28–29
defined, xiv, 145
development of, 26–27
double-dominant profiles, 35
EDBA sequence's importance,
  33–34
integrated implementation of,
  38–39
integrated outcomes of, 28
key initiatives improved via, 29–30
leadership skills improved via,
  40–42
measuring your knowledge
  of, 129–32
new leaders acclimated via, 29
overview, xiii–xiv
preferences and abilities iden-
  tified through, 94
priority setting via, 30
quadruple-dominant profiles, 36
single-dominant profiles, 34
as socio-systematic, 31–32
socio-systematic velocity
  increases via, 26–33
SP survey results, 32–33
starting a project with, 25
step-by-step process of, 27–28
transitions between phases
  managed via, 30

triple-dominant profiles, 36
velocity increases via, 28
visionaries, 37–38
for work streams, 87–88
staff expansion, 115
stakeholders
  analyses of, 53
  Envision step's importance to, 47
  insights about, xvii, 12
  role in transformation strategy, 86
standardization, 76
Stanford Research Institute, 53
Strategic Profiling (SP), 31–36,
  144–45
  See also SP-AP
subjective knowledge. See Envision
subjective work. See Activate
supply chains, 145
SWOT analysis, 53
system dynamics, 145
systems, 81, 145

tact, 105
Taylor, Frederick, 5, 7–8, 144
technological progress, 4
The Theory of Constraints
  (Goldratt), 83
time, value of, 60–61
TMOs (transformation-
  management offices), 87, 145
trademarks, 111
transformation-management
  offices (TMOs), 87, 145

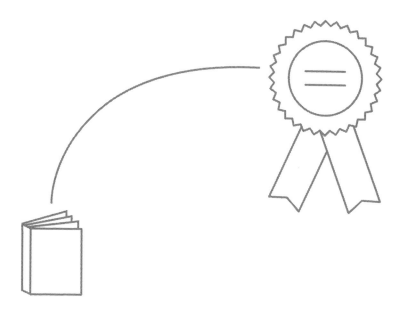

From Comprehension to Certification

Are you ready to take your expertise to the next level? You're invited to take part in *The Velocity Advantage eLearning* program — a fun and easy way to master the art and science of successfully implementing cross-functional initiatives.

In only 2½ hours you can earn your Velocity Advantage certification and join our community of experts.

It's easy to get started.
SP-AP.com

Made in the USA
Middletown, DE
06 May 2019